HADRAT BILAL

(May Allah Be Pleased With Him)

The First Muadhdhin of Islam

'Abbas Mahmood al-'Akkad

KITAB BHAVAN
New Delhi-110002

KITAB BHAVAN
Publishers, Distributors, Exporters & Importers
1784, Kalan Mahal, Darya Ganj
New Delhi-110002 [India]

Phones : (91-11) 3274686, 3277392, 3277393
3258006, 3258007, 3258008
E-Mail : nasri@nda.vsnl.net.in
Website : http://www.kitabbhavan.com
Fax : (91-11) 3263383

ISBN 81-7151-191-0
Code No. H00110

Ist Publsihed in India 1994
Second Edition 1998

Printed & Published in India by :
Nusrat Ali Nasri for Kitab Bhavan
1784, Kalan Mahal, Darya Ganj
New Delhi-110002 [India]

CONTENTS

PREFACE

It gives me great pleasure in presenting this book, a biography of one of the close companions of Prophet Muhammad (peace and blessings of Allah be upon him), Bilal b. Ribah (may Allah be pleased with him), who also had the unique privilege of being the first *Muadhdhin* of Islam.

This is not an exact translation but an adaptation from an Arabic book under the title 'Bilal Ibn Ribah, The *Muadhdhin* of the Prophet', by 'Abbas Mahmood al-'Akkad. Some historical facts have been added, while matters of dispute have been eliminated, still maintaining the authenticity of the facts about his life.

My aim is to present to the readers the true character of Haḍrat Bilal (may Allah be pleased with him), who rose to unparallelled heights from the depth of slavery due entirely to his singleminded devotion to Islam and complete submission to the Will of Allah, in addition to his exemplary dedication to the Prophet Muhammad (peace and blessings of Allah be upon him).

The religion of Islam provides guaranteed equality, freedom and justice to all, irrespective of color, race or creed. Haḍrat Bilal's life, without doubt, is a living example of this unique aspect of Islam, unmatched by any other religion, in theory or in practice.

May Almighty Allah grant us the guidance to follow in his footsteps and give us the courage, wisdom, strength and steadfastness of this great Muslim, a very close confidant of the Prophet of Islam, Ameen!

FOREWORD

This book is a brief life sketch of Hadrat Bilal (Allah be pleased with him), the first Mu'adhdhin of the Prophet of Islam (peace and blessings of Allah be upon him).

Hadrat Bilal (Allah be pleased with him) was a Negro slave before the advent of Islam. He was one of the first seven converts to Islam. After accepting Islam Hadrat Bilal (Allah be pleased with him) was persecuted severely by his master. Hadrat Abū Bakr as-Siddiq (Allah be pleased with him) bought him and emancipated him. Thereafter Hadrat Bilal (Allah be pleased with him) remained in constant attendance on the Holy Prophet (peace and blessings of Allah be upon him) and was very near and dear to him. He was selected by the Holy Prophet (peace and blessings of Allah be upon him) as the first Mu'adhdhin of Islam. Hadrat Bilal (Allah be pleased with him) was one of the closest Companions of the Holy Prophet (peace and blessings of Allah be upon him) and this closeness rose him to the highest position of honour from a persecuted slave.

Muhammad Ikram Siddiqi

HADRAT BILAL

(May Allah be pleased with him)

There is a consensus of opinion among the historians that Hadrat Bilal (Allah be pleased with him) was not a pure Abyssinian. He was, however, born of the Abyssinian mother. His father was an Arab. Bilal's complexion was dark-brown. His body was slim and tall, with a prominent chest. His hair was thick and his cheeks were thin.

These features are found in the races of the *Saud* and the *Samis.* These races mostly lived between Abyssinia and Yemen from ancient times. His features were not identical with those of the *Zang* or the sons of *Sam.* His complexion was black and his hair was thick; but his nose was not snub, nor was his hair curly. This betrayed that he came of parents belonging to two different races. Some have opined that he pronunciated the letter 'S' as 'Sh' like the Saud. But authentic scholars have refuted this view. They have supplemented their refutation by the fact that he used to announce for prayers (i.e. he said *Adhan*) and the announcement (Adhnan) contained both "Seen" (س) and "Swad" (ص). Were he to pronounce "S" as "Sh", he would have not been appointed as announcer for prayers *(Mua'dh-dhin).*

There is a difference of opinion about his birth-place. Some historians claimed that he was born at

Mecca, whereas the others were of the opinion that he was born in Sarat. The latter view seems to be more plausible for Sarat is a town near Yemen and Abyssinia, where there can be found a mixed race. It is also stated that he went to that place once to get married.

Like his birth-place, there is much difference of opinion in regard to the date of his birth. The most preferable view is that he was born about 43 years before *Hijra* and according to another view he was born 53 years before *Hijra*. His father and mother were well-known figures. His father's name was Ribah and his mother was called Hamama. Some of the high-headed Quraish called him *Ibn Sauda* by way of contempt. It is likely that his mother was slave-girl from Sarat or Mecca. If this view be taken as correct, it would mean that she was not born at Sarat.

Some of the European historians are of the view that he learnt the first lesson of *Tauhid*, as was preached by the Christians of Abyssinia, from his mother.

It is, therefore, held that he readily responded to the call of Muhammad (peace and blessings of Allah be upon him) when he came out with the message of Oneness of Allah. But it is not correct because the Abyssinians considered Christianity nearest to idolatry and they did not welcome the call of Muhammad (peace and blessings of Allah be upon him) towards *Tauhid* vehemently. If they had been the standard-bearers of *Tauhid* how could they have opposed Allah's Messenger (peace blessings of Allah be upon him) and the message preached by him tooth and nail? They should have readily accepted his invitation.

Some other historians have written that Hadrat Bilal (Allah be pleased with him) had a brother whose name was Khalid and he was also called as Abu Rouwaiha – his patronymic name. Some of the authentic narrations prove that Abu Rouwaiha was not his real brother but he was his brother in faith like the brotherhood established by Allah's Messenger (peace and blessings of Allah be upon him) among his companions on his migration to Medina. It is also claimed that he had a sister Ghafra by name who was the slave girl of 'Abdullah .

Hadrat Bilal (Allah be pleased with him) was brought up at Mecca in a well-known Quraishite tribe, Abu Jamah. It is interesting to note that Abu Mahdhura, one of three announcers of *Adhan* of the Holy Prophet, was also brought up in that very tribe. These three announcers of *Adhan* were, Bilal, Abu Mahdhura and 'Amr b. Umm-i-Kalthum. It cannot be said whether it was a mere chance or it was due to their interest in melody and harmony of voice that two of the three announcers were brought up in this tribe. During the days of ignorance, the members of this tribe drew out lots with the help of an arrow. They were also experts in reading the lines of hands. When there was a dispute between Banu 'Abd Dar and Banu 'Abdul Manaf, the members of this tribe sided with Banu 'Abd Dar, with the result that there was a perpetual conflict between this tribe and Banu 'Abd Munaf. Hadrat Bilal (Allah be pleased with him) had a natural hatred against the customs and practices of the days of ignorance because of his being brought up in the tribe of Banu Jamah. He witnessed day and night that deceit had become the second nature of the people of Banu 'Abd Munaf and the members of this tribe were devoid of kind-heartedness, good morals and sympathy. This hatred became the reason of his accepting Islam.

It has not so far been ascertained with authenticity as to who amongst this tribe of Banu Jamah, was the master of Bilal and his father. Some assert that he had been the slave of a noble woman of that tribe whereas others claim that the widow of the relative of Abu Jahl was his mistress. Some authors claim that he was the slave of Umaiyya b. Khalaf.

Historians are, however, agreed that it was Abu Bakr Siddique (May Allah be plea ed with him) who secured emancipation for him after he had seen him being the victim of the worst torment for his embracing Islam. So he bought him for 5 *Uqiyas* of Gold. Some say he bought him for 7 *Uqiyas* and some say he paid 9 *Uqiyas*. It is narrated by some historians that when the transaction was being paid, the master of Bilal increased the price and Haḍrat Abu Bakr Siddique (May Allah be pleased with him) said to him," Even if you raise this price to 1,000 *Uqiyas*, I will definitely buy him".

Some historians are of the view that Haḍrat Abu Bakr Siddique (May Allah be pleased with him) exchanged him for another slave who was most stout and firm of his slaves but this narration seems to be doubtful. It is inconceivable that Harḍat Abu Bakr Siddique (May Allah be pleased with him) could have given a Muslim to the Polytheists for perpetrating atrocities upon him. This appears something impossible keeping in view the temperament of Haḍrat Abu Bakr Siddique (May Allah be pleased with him). There is no gainsaying the fact that Hadrat

Abu Bakr Siddique (May Allah be pleased with him) bought Bilal at the command of Allah's Apostle (peace and blessings of Allah be upon him) and he offered him half of the price in order to share the cost with him so that it might mitigate the burden of feeding him and that of other weak Muslims. But Hadrat Abu Bakr Siddique (May Allah be pleased with him) who had helped many a weak person like him, said; "Allah's Messenger (peace and blessings of Allah be upon you), I have emancipated Bilal". He then appointed Bilal as his own Storekeeper and later he was made to serve in that very capacity Allah's Apostle (peace and blessings of Allah be upon him) and then he was appointed as the announcer of *Adhan* after the the call of prayer had been instituted. Bilal found a relief from the torment that the masters inflicted on their slaves but he did not secure immunity from the torture to which even free men amongst the Muslims had been subjected, especially from the torture inflicted on such weak persons as had no backing or had no power to demand blood-wit.

The Polytheists persecuted the Muslims with all the tortures they could possibly perpetrate. At last they decided to kill the Holy Prophet (may peace and blessings be upon him). They convened an assembly of all the tribes so that they might come at a decision to put the Holy Prophet to death jointly. They considered that the Hashemite would not be strong enough to wage war with everyone of them and take vengeance from every tribe individually. At this juncture, the Holy prophet (peace and blessings be upon him) granted his companions permission to migrate. Hence Bilal, along with other companions, migrated to Medina, but the memory of Mecca never faded from his mind. When the Prophet (peace be upon him) and his companion, Abu Bakr Siddique, reached Medina it presented the spectacle of a parched land; but it was far milder than the persecution which the Muslims had undergone in Mecca. Haḍrat Abu Bakr Siddique, Amir b. Fahria, and Bilal lived in the same house and all of them suffered from Malaria. When the fever aggravated, Bilal (Allah be pleased with him) would recite the following verses lying in the compound of his house:–

> Would that I had known that a time would come when I would pass a night in the Vale of Mecca, surrounded by pastures of Azkhir and Jalil;
> Would that a day must come when I shall drink from the spring of Majna and my eyes would see the hills of Shama and Tufail.

These verses reveal that despite having suffered all sorts of hardships and severe torments there, Haḍrat Bilal's heart was full of longing for the place where he had spent the time of his childhood and where he had been living upto that time. As in Mecca, so in Medina, Haḍrat Bilal (Allah be pleased with him) could not endure separation from the Holy Prophet (peace and blessings of Allah be on him). Haḍrat Bilal (Allah be pleased with him) was constantly in attendance upon the Holy Prophet (peace be on him) in all the holy wars that took place during the Prophet's lifetime and in the course of all journeys he undertook. It was for this reason that the honour of being the first *Mua 'dh dhin* (Announcer for Prayer) in the mosque of Medina, in the construction of which the Holy Prophet himself participated, was conferred upon Hadrat Bilal (Allah be pleased with him), an office which he continued to perform till the Holy Prophet (peace and blessings of Allah be on him), left for his Heavenly abode.

He enjoyed preference over all the *Mua'dh dhins* (announcers for prayers) during the Prophet's lifetime, the ground of this preference being his precedence in embracing Islam, his sonorous voice and his excellent utterance. If he had taken lead in embracing Islam, it was better than other distinctions should fall to his lot.

When Bilal recited the call *(adhan)* and wished that the Holy Prophet should know that he had announced for prayer (i.e. recited *adhan),* he would stand by the door of the Prophet's Chamber and would shout حي على الصلوة (Hasten to the prayer), حي على الفلاح Hasten to well-being), الصلوة يا رسول الله (Prayer O Messenger of Allah). When the Holy Prophet (peace and blessings of Allah be on him) would come for the prayer, Bilal used to say Iquama (اقامه) before the service commenced.

One distinct aspect of his announcement for prayer *(adhan)* was that he recited the *adhan* when the sun was yet pale and did not set in completely but he deferred the *Iqama* a bit; or mostly he deferred it a bit, but he never missed the time of *adhan*.

Sometimes he prefaced the call for prayer by reciting a verse in melody, descriptive of his helpless state and seeking repentance and mercy from Allah. One out of many such verses is as follows:-

"How aggrieved is the mother of Bilal for him as he was bathed in the blood of his brow." Before the mosque was constructed, on occasions of Eid and Namaz-i-Istisqa عيد،صلوٰة الاستسقا, Bilal (Pleasure of Allah be on him), holding a spear, used to walk ahead of the Prophet (peace be on him); and used to pitch the spear in the ground one or two yards away from the place where the Holy Prophet (peace and blessings of Allah be on him) wished to lead the prayer service. The spear was one of the three gifts sent in homage to the Holy Prophet (peace be on him) by the King of Abyssinia. The Holy Prophet (peace be on him) had kept one for himself and had gifted the other two spears to Hadrat 'Ali b Abi Talib and Hadrat 'Umar b.al-Khatab (Allah be pleased with them); Hadrat Bilal (Allah's pleasure be on him) was honoured with keeping the Prophet's spear throughout his life time. He carried the spear with him on the occasions of Eid and Namaz-i-Istisqa and pitched that where the prayer was to be offered. Historians have recorded that Bilal (Allah be pleased with him) continued to perform this function in the august reign of Hadrat Abu Bakr Siddique (Allah be pleased with him). In the reigns of Hadrat 'Umar and Hadrat 'Uthman (Allah be pleased with both of them) this office was conferred on Sa'd Qarz according to the instruction of Hadrat Bilal.

The spear was preserved for a longtime and a functionary used to walk ahead of the emperors holding the spear in hand after the Caliphs. On arriving at Medina, the Holy Prophet (peace and blessings of Allah be on him) established a bond of fraternity between the emigrants *(Mahajirin)* and the *Ansar* (helpers). The Holy Prophet (peace be on him) declared Hadrat Bilal (pleasure of Allah be on him) the brother of Khalid Abu Rouwaiha al-Khaith'mi. Some authorities report that brotherhood was established between Bilal and 'Ubaida b. al-Harith b. Abdul Muttalib; or between him and abu 'Ubaida b Jarrah (Allah be pleased with them), but this does not appear to be true. The first view is more valid that close bond of brotherhood had subsisted between Haḍrat Bilal and Abu Rouwaiha (Allah be pleased with them) till the end. It is reported in the traditions that the Holy Prophet (peace be on him) paid close attention to the education and training of Haḍrat Bilal (Allah be pleased with him). Once the Holy Prophet (peace and blessings of Allah be upon him) said, "O Bilal! the best deed that a believer can perform is to struggle for the cause of Allah". Concerning humility, the Prophet (peace be on him) taught him.

> "O Bilal! Live always in humility and with contentment and die with those who feel contented."

Off and on, the Holy Prophet (peace and blessings of Allah be on him) gave advice to Bilal (Allah be pleased with him) regarding distribution of the surplus wealth with him. He would say "Bilal! a quantity of wealth has accumulated with me. I do not wish to keep it. Take it and give it away to the needy, so that my heart may be alleviated from a burden."

As a matter of fact, the Holy Prophet (peace and blessings of Allah be on him) intended to instruct Haḍrat Bilal (Allah be pleased with him) by example that a man should cultivate the virtue of contentment in life and abstain from storing wealth. Bilal observed scrupulously all the instructions and precedents of the Holy Prophet (peace and blessings of Allah be on him) and proved himself a true follower and a faithful devotee of the Prophet (peace be on him) till the close of his life.

Once during the course of a Divine Revelation, the sight of Paradise was opened up before the Holy Prophet (peace and blessings of Allah be on him). At this moment the sound of Bilal's footsteps came to the ears of the Holy Prophet (peace and blessings of Allah be on him). At the close of prayer - service, the Holy Prophet (peace be on him) observed: "Bilal, tell me which of your deed in Islam, you hope, will fetch you greatest blessing of Allah,. I have heard tonight the sound of your steps ahead of myself." Hadrat Bilal's modesty on that occasion was remarkable. He made no mention of his piety and contentment, nor of his struggles for the cause of Allah. He did not recount the hardships and torments that he had to bear in the way of True Faith and which he had endured with singular patience and fortitude, nor did he hint at his virtues of obedience and true devotion. He merely said, "I have performed no extraordinary deed in my life as a Muslim for which Allah may repay me with this special bounty. Yet I admit it is my practice that whenever I perform ablution during any part of the day and night, I observe supererogatory prayer.

Hadrat Bilal (Allah be pleased with him) performed the duties of an attendant upon the Holy Prophet (peace and blessings of Allah be on him) in all circumstances, during journeys and stay in Camp, in war and peace, but the Holy Prophet never treated him like a servant of the Knights or monarchs. He was in constant attendance on the Holy Prophet (peace and blessings of Allah be on him) day and night, because he derived delight from his sight, love and kindness.

Bilal, too, expressed deep devotion, which sprang spontaneously on one occasion or the other, for his master and leader. He could not bear in peace the slightest discomfort of the Holy Prophet (peace and blessings of Allah be on him) and was ready at all hours to respond to his Master's (peace be on him) Call. On a journey when the sun grew intensely hot at noon, Hadrat Bilal (Allah be pleased with him) without waiting for an order, used to raise a cloth canopy over the head of the Holy Prophet (peace and blessings of Allah be on him). In war Bilal (Allah be pleased with him) used to pitch a tent at some distance from the battle-field wherefrom the Holy Prophet (peace and blessings of Allah be on him) watched the situation of the battle. Throughout the battle Bilal kept running errands between the Prophet's Camp and the battle-field, bearing communications, orders and instructions from the Holy Prophet (peace be on him) to the the troops. Neither adversity nor danger could separate him from the Holy Prophet (peace be on him). After eight year' exile when the Holy Prophet (peace and blessings of Allah be on him) made a victorious entry into the city of Mecca, he ordered Bilal to ascend the top of Ka'ba and recite the call to prayer. He recited the call to prayer (*adhan*). As soon as he had uttered the words "Ash hadu 'an - La - illaha, il' lallahu" (I bear witness that there is no god exept Allah.), the hearts of the infidels were stricken with remorse and pain. Some infidels were even moved to say, "Tis well that my father is dead or the sound of these words would have been hard to bear for him." When Bilal's call to prayer was over, the Holy Prophet (peace and blessings of Allah be on him) entered the Shrine of Ka'ba accompanied by three men only : (1) Uthman b Talha, the Key-bearer if the Shrine of Ka'ba, (2) Usama b Zaid, the adopted son of the Holy Prophet, and (3) Bilal (Allah be pleased with them). Bilal performed the duty of reciting the call to prayer continously during the lifetime of the Holy Prophet (peace and blessings of Allah be on him). He recited the call for prayers for a few days only after the Holy Prophet had left his Heavenly home and then excused himself from performing the office. Even in the face of persistent entreaties to resume the office, he remained adamant. The reason was that as soon as he uttered the aphorism, "I bear witness that Muhammad is the Prophet of Allah," he missed the presence of the Holy Prophet (peace and blessings of Allah be on him) and burst into uncontrollable tears. His audience too, stricken with grief, broke down. The mosque of the Prophet (peace be on him) on these occasions turned into a House of Bereavement. Separated from his beloved master, Bilal felt oppressed in the environs of Medina. Although at this time he was over sixty years of age, he resolved to forsake his peaceful life in Medina and devote the rest of his days to Holy war in far-away lands. He applied to Hadrat Abu Bakr Siddique (May Allah be pleased with him) to relieve him of duty of calling for prayer (*adhan*) and grant him leave to go to Syria with the soldiers (*Mujahidin*). On his persistent requests, Hadrat Abu Bakr (Allah be pleased with him) was constrained to grant him leave. He, then participated in a number of battles the details of which are not known. He went to his small piece of land in the environs of Damascus, which he cultivated and lived on the produce yielded by it. After this nothing was heard about him but he was seen when he announced the call for prayer (*adhan*) for the Caliph 'Umar on the request of the eminent companions of the Holy Prophet and their successors (*Tabi 'in*) and on the day when Khalid b Walid was to render his account before Abu 'Ubaida. According to the most authentic opinion, Bilal (May Allah be pleased with him) was of the same age as Haḍrat Abu Bakr was.

He was seventy when he died. It is held by some that he died of epidemic like Plague in 'Umwas; and it is said that it was the year 20 of *Hijra*. On his death-bed he rejoiced at the prospect of meeting his beloved master (peace be on him) and his companions. When his wife wept bitterly and cried out by his side he comforted her with these words:-

> "Why do you weep? I am looking forward to seeing the Holy Prophet (peace be on him) and other old companions after such a long separation. Allah-willing I shall meet them all tomorrow."

Bilal (Allah be pleased with him) expired in Damascus and was buried near Bab-al-Saghir. His tomb is upto this day the favourite resort of crowds of visitors, high and low, who come to offer homage at his grave. Bilal was held in great esteem by the companions (Allah be pleased with them) and their successors. An estimate of their reverence for him may be made from the following historical episode. When during his caliphate, Haḍrat 'Umar (Allah be pleased with him) went on a tour of Syria, Haḍrat Bilal (Allah be pleased with him) came to see him in Damascus. Some of those present on this occasion suggested that Bilal (Allah be pleased with him) should recite the call to prayer. Haḍrat 'Umar (Allah be pleased with him) approved of the idea and expressed his own personal desire to hear Bilal's rendition of the call to Prayer.

So when the time of prayer approached, Bilal in deference to the wish of the righteous caliph stood up and began to announce the prayer-Call. No sooner was the call uttered than there arose voices of grief and lamentation. Venerable Companions, including Haḍrat' Umar (Allah be pleased with them) himself burst into tears till the tears from their eyes drenched their beards. The common people were amazed at the scene of a mosque suddenly turning into a bereaved congregation of piteously crying and grievously lamenting people on the utterance of prayer-Call by an individual. But Bilal's recital of the Prayer-Call was quite unlike the utterance of the Call by an ordinary person. Bilal's recital evoked memories of the time when the Holy Prophet (peace and blessings of Allah be on him) used to grace the *Masjid-i-Nabvi* with his (peace be on him) august presence and Bilal announced the Prayer-Call five times a day in his presence. On the passing away of the Holy Prophet (peace and blessings of Allah be on him) Bilal's voice had also been denied to the Muslims. When after such a long interval the voice of Bilal (Allah be pleased with him) once again came to their ears, it recalled to their minds the period of the Holy Prophet (peace and blessings of Allah be on him) and the Muslims fell into uncontrollable weeping. Haḍrat Bilal (Allah be pleased with him) was revered, more so because the Holy Prophet (peace and blessings of Allah be on him) had borne singular affection towards him throughout his life. Among all the Companions of the Holy Prophet (peace and blessings be on him). Bilal was the most beloved of the prophet. The Holy Prophet (peace and blessings of Allah be on him) not only looked after Bilal's religious training, but Bilal's worldly needs also were the object of constant care of the Holy Prophet (peace be on him). Traditions relate that Bilal's marriage had been arranged by the Holy Prophet (peace and blessings of Allah be on him). It is stated that the sons of Abu-al-Bukair came to the presence of the Holy Prophet (peace and blessings of Allah be on him) and submitted. "Prophet of Allah, (peace be on you) find a match for our sister". The Holy Prophet (peace and blessings of Allah be on him) observed, "Why don't you marry her to Bilal." Hearing this they went back. After a few days they returned and repeated the same request. The Holy Prophet (peace and blessings of Allah be on him) again observed, "Why don't you marry her to Bilal." Hearing this, they returned. Later they came with the same request for the third time. This time also the Holy Prophet (peace be on him) remarked, "Why don't you marry her to Bilal? He is an inmate of Paradise. You should marry your sister to him." So having heard the Prophet's (peace be on him) affirmation thrice, they married their sister to Bilal (Allah be pleased with him). Bilal took more wives after this marriage. Qatadah reports that he had married a beduoin female of the tribe of Banu Zuhra. Traditions also record that the name of one of his wives was Hind-ul-Khulania and she belonged to the Yemen. Abu Ishaque relates that Bilal (Allah be pleased with him had no issue from these marriages. Bilal (Allah be pleased with him) left no legacy in the form of material wealth, yet he left a spiritual memorial which is unique in the world and that is *Adhan* (the Prayer – Call). The Call to Prayer has been recited continuously in the world of Islam for the last fourteen centuries, and so soon as the Call is pronounced it recalls to mind the memory of the First *Muadh'dhin* (Caller to Prayer) of Islam Hadrat Bilal b Ribah, Allah be pleased with him.

BILAL'S

ACCEPTANCE OF ISLAM

The two attributes of Faith are that it should not be confined to a particular person and that it should not be subject to any expediency. When a man is convinced in his own mind of the truth of certain principles, but does not or cannot convert others to these principles, then he cannot be said to have attained faith.

Similarly when unalterable beliefs are surrendered in the face of timely expediency, even though hundreds of people may be involved in this act of surrender, no person in the world will adjudge them as people of faith and excellence. Such people will be viewed as bearing wavering convictions and weak faith. Faith and expediency are antithetic. It is impossible that the two should combine in one person. The truly pious man sacrifices his timely expediencies in the way of Faith and in the face of severe hardships and dreadful tortures holds steadfast to his faith. Faith is far above expediencies and a man can attain real dignity only by virtue of displaying the highest degree of Faith and Excellence.

It can be said about Bilal (Allah be pleased with him) without any trace of doubt that he had attained the highest degree of Faith and no form of torture or threat could deflect his steps from the path of perseverence in Faith. Bilal (Allah be pleased with him) was among the first eight persons who had responded to the call of the Holy Prophet (peace and blessings of Allah be on him). The other seven were Haḍrat Khadija, Haḍrat Abu Bakr Siddique, Haḍrat 'Ali, Haḍrat 'Ammar, his mother Sumiyya, Haḍrat Suhaib and Hadrat Miqdad (Allah be pleased with them).

The historians relate that because of the great personal influence of Haḍrat Abu Bakr in Mecca and for fear of antagonising his tribe who supported him infidels dared not molest him. But apart from him the other Muslims were weak and helpless. They had no supporters or sympathisers. So the pagans inflicted endless tortures on them. Tying ropes to the legs of the Muslims, the infidels dragged them on the stony ground of Mecca. They stripped the Muslims naked and throwing them on the burning sand, placed heavy stones on their bodies. They forced the Muslims to stand in the blazing Sun wearing Coats of mail. By inflicting such unspeakable tortures on the Muslims, the infidels succeeded in coercing some men to make statements which suited the infidels' purpose. But Bilal (Allah be pleased with him) displayed unflinching fortitude, patience and perseverence. The infidels employed all sorts of strategies to divert Bilal from his faith in Islam.

There was no form of threat which was not held out to Bilal (Allah be pleased with him) and there was no form of torture which the infidels did not execute on him. But in the face of all this Bilal held firm to his creed. "None has the right to be worshipped but Allah."

The book 'Tabqat Ibn Sa'd, contains some details of the atrocities perpetrated on Haḍrat Bilal (Allah be pleased with him). We produce below some relevant excerpts from this book, which describe the sacrifices made by Bilal (Allah be pleased with him) in the way of Faith.

'Urwa b Zubair reported that Bilal belonged to that group of the pious who were very weak, poor and helpless by worldly standards. When he accepted Islam, the infidels subjected him to a series of torments so that he might succumb to renunciation of his faith, but Bilal (Allah be pleased with him) did not utter a syllable which suited the views of the infidels.

Bilal's (Allah be pleased with him) master Umaiyya bin Khalaf was his greatest tormetor. When the affliction caused by the tortures deepened, Bilal would utter 'Ahad, Ahad, (Allah is one, Allah is one.) The tormentors demanded of him, "Repeat what we say." But he would reply, "My tongue is not suited to utter your sayings."

It is reported that Bilal was seized by his masters. They threw him down and flung a stone and a cow-hide over him. They said to him, "Your Gods are al-Lat and al 'Uzza. Testify your faith in them." But Bilal continued to say 'Ahad, Ahad, (Allah is one, Allah is one.) At last when the torments reached extremity, Haḍrat Abu Bakr (Allah be pleased with him) came to Bilal's rescue and said to his masters, "How long ye people will oppress this man?" So saying Abu Bakr (Allah be pleased with him) bought Bilal (Allah be pleased with him) on payment of

Seven *Uqiya* (equivalent to 23 grams of gold) and declared him a free man. It is recorded in *Tabaqat* that Abu Jahl came during the night and began to abuse Sumiyyah (May Allah be pleased with her). He attacked upon her with a spear and killed her. She was the first lady to attain martyrdom in Islam. Hadrat Bilal considered his life of no importance in regard to his love for Allah, he could not therefore afford to renounce his faith with the threat of tortures. The infidels tied a rope round his neck and urged the urchins to drag him to and fro between the two hills of Mecca. Yet under this severe torment Bilal's tongue repeated only one word 'Ahad, Ahad.' (Allah is one, Allah is one.). Thereupon the infidels gave him a severe beating and stretching him on the burning sand they would place a heavy stone over his body, still Bilal uttered nothing save the creed "Allah is one, Allah is one."

By enduring all sorts of humiliations and unbearable atrocities in the way of love for the Divine and devotion to the Righteous Faith, Hadrat Bilal set an example which will serve as a beacon light for the seekers after Truth and Righteousness till the end of this world. As mentioned earlier, Hadrat Bilal (Allah be pleased with him) was included among those who had made an immediate affirmative response on hearing the call of the Holy Prophet (peace and blessings of Allah be on him) to the belief in one Allah. They knew well the consequence of renouncing idol worship and offering devotion and prostration to the one Allah, the Lord of Heaven. They were not ignorant of the various tortures and horrible atrocities that they would have to endure as a result of renouncing faith in Polytheism, yet so deep was the imprint of the righteous life and unparralelled good morals of the Holy Prophet (peace and blessings of Allah be on him) upon their hearts that no degree of savage oppression and violence, nor the most fearful threats could blot it out. It is due to this inner strength of character that they unreservedly accepted the call of the Holy Prophet (peace and blessings of Allah be on him) as soon as it came to them.

No one succeeded in attaining such sublime estate in Faith and knowledge as these fortunate few. They did not embrace Islam with the selfish motive of securing freedom from their inhuman masters or obtaining some relief from the stringent conditions of slavery. It is not difficult to understand from a study of the circumstances prevailing at that time that it was a critical period for the early Muslims.

Besides the slaves, the other converts to Islam who belonged to various tribes of Arabia enjoyed no better status than slaves. The citizens of Mecca subjected these people to extremes of violence and oppression and forced them to renounce their faith in Islam, by means of all the stringent measures they could use. In view of these conditions how could these poor Muslims, whose own plight was miserable and who daily feared for their lives, be expected to secure emancipation for the slaves who accepted Islam. It is also unreasonable to suppose that the slaves had been tempted to embrace Islam by the prospect of obtaining relief from the rigours of slave life. Had this been their motive for conversion to Islam, they would have waited till their masters, attracted by Islamic teachings, had entered the fold of Islam and gave them a better deal under the impress of the moral principles of Islam; or the slaves could have waited till a majority of the Meccans became Muslims and exerted pressure on the cruel masters on behalf of the slaves. At that time, by far the larger number of Muslim converts were those who were poor, helpless and weak, powerless to defend themselves from the atrocious assaults of the Polytheists. How could these people promise the slaves protection from the torments of their owners? If it be admitted that the slaves accepted Islam because Islam accords equal rights to slave and free man and impressed by this principle they had transferred their allegiance to the Holy Prophet (peace and blessings of Allah be on him), the question may be rightly asked what, then, was the reason for the free men to embrace the fold of Islam? It is an indubitable fact that the slaves and free persons did not enjoy equality of status before the advent of Islam, and the free persons viewed slaves with hatred and contempt and meted out disgraceful treatment to them. After all why did the free persons who deemed themselves in every way superior to the slaves, feel impelled to accept a creed which envisaged equality of all human beings and sought to make all men, slaves and free persons, to stand at par?. If slaves like Bilal and Suhaib (Allah be pleased with them) had been tempted to embrace Islam by their ambition to enjoy equal with noblemen like Abu Bakr, Hamza, 'Ali and 'Umar (Allah be pleased with them), then what expediency impelled these noble men to degrade themselves and accept equal status with the poor, helpless, humble and destitute slaves and thus bring upon themselves the taunts and rancour of the

Quraish? As a matter of fact neither the slaves had accepted Islam on the ground that Islam had promised equal footing for the slaves and free men, nor was the ideal of equality of human beings put forth to the world by the Holy Prophet (peace and blessings of Allah be on him) the real cause for the acceptance of faith by the free people. For if we lend credence to this proposition, we cannot escape the conclusion that self-interest provided the motive for various groups to enter the fold of Islam. On the contrary, in the first place, faith and expediency are antithetic and cannot co-exist in one heart. Secondly, the great sacrifices made in the way of Islam by the first converts and the heroic manner in which they gave lives for the mission of the Apostle of Allah (peace and blessings be on him) furnish a clear proof that their conversion to Islam was not motivated by self-interest. It is a sign of true faith that when a man accepts a creed believing it to be righteous, he holds to it with rock like firmness under all forms of calamity, hardship and trial and puts little value upon his life in defense of his belief. It is a matter of deep reflection that how a man who was stretched on the burning sand of the desert and tortured by placing of heavy stones upon his chest in punishment for his conversion to the new faith and was by these means forced to abandon faith — how can this man bring upon himself such fearful reparations on the chance that he will obtain freedom from his cruel owners by accepting a new religion? Can it be imagined that this man who uttered only Allah is one, Allah is one and no form of torture could deter him from repeating this aphorism, did not have the discretion to make a comparison between his hereditary religion (idolatry) and Islam and possessed no further knowledge of Islam than that its teaching is confined to providing a better deal for the slaves?

A brief statement of the atrocities to which the infidels of Mecca subjected Bilal (Allah be pleased with him) in retaliation for his refusal to worship the idols and for his frank espousal of the creed of one Allah has been given in the preceding pages. In reality the severity of these tortures did not fall short of hurling the man into the throes of death. The Polytheists would have felt no compunction in actually killing him, had they not prevented by the consideration that in so doing, they would lose a profitable chattel. In any case, had not Abu Bakr (Allah be pleased with him) bought his freedom, despair would have driven the infidels to assassinate him too, as they had done Haḍrat Ammar's mother Sumiyyah (Allah be pleased with them) before him.

The above circumstances clearly establish the fact that Bilal (Allah be pleased with him) had not embraced Islam with the motive of securing relief from the severity of the torments of slave life; on the contrary he had invited upon himself torments of double even treble intensity by entering the fold of Islam.

Upon reflection it will be found that the savage atrocities perpetrated on Bilal (Allah be pleased with him) were beyond the endurance of any human being. Haḍrat 'Ammar shared the same lot, but he also endured all the sufferings attained that sublime state of Faith which can be achieved by a fortunate few His faith was like pure gold, unalloyed by any covetousness or sensuous desires. He was the type of person who adopts a faith with a sincere heart and then cannot bear to renounce it under any circumstances. He had only one purpose in view and that was to win the favour of Allah. To this end he offered all forms of sacrifices. Death was trivial to him, as we have mentioned earlier. He continued to take part in the holy wars upto the age of ninety when he finally fell a martyr in the battle of Saffrin. Nevertheless, in spite of possessing such a true faith, he was unable to sustain the terrific tortures of the Polytheists.

In contrast Haḍrat Bilal (Allah be pleased with him) endured these atrocities with remarkable patience and fortitude. Afflicted by these torments, Bilal (Allah be pleased with him) did not even give out a cry of pain. If Bilal (Allah be pleased with him) had hoped for gaining any advantage from accepting Islam, he would sooner have given up any thought of obtaining them under the pain of terrible tortures. But the Lord had illumined his heart with the light of faith. Hence no amount of force in the world proved sufficient to deter him from the faith which he had adopted with a sincere heart, after careful deliberation.

History bears witness to the fact that in the initial stages of the advent of Islam it were the slaves, by and large, who attained the privilege of responding to the Call of *Tauhid* (One Allah). Those who conceived themselves as superiors and honourable in most part kept aloof and hence were deprived of this privilege. Expediency at each step barred the way of the free people of Quraish to accept Islam. Some feared loss of reputation by embracing Islam. Some apprehended complete financial ruination as a result of their acceptance of Islam. Some feared the enmity of their whole tribe; others were consumed by the fear of opposition from their relations. But the poor slaves were free from all these shackles. They did not worry about losing any reputation, nor were they afraid of loss of business. They had no apprehension of exciting anger in their tribe nor did they fear any alienation from their kith and kin. It was in accord with their nature to accept the Truth unreservedly. They embraced Islam in perfect sincerity and with true heart and endured all the hardships and afflictions for the sake of Islam with poise and dignity. Like other slaves, Haḍrat Bilal's heart was also filled with the sentiments of affection, sincerity, obedience and devotion. The mirror of his heart carried no taint of rancour. Hence as soon as he heard the clarion Call for the acceptance of faith in one Allah and the equality of all human beings issued by the noblest scion of the most respectable family (Banu Hashim), Bilal (Allah be pleased with him) at once made an affirmative response. The thought must have crossed his mind like a flash of lightening that the person who wanted to liquidate class differences in order to put the master and slave on a footing of equality and the man who belonged to the noblest class in Mecca, yet was a staunch champion of the equality of all human beings, could not but be an extraordinary human being. It was unbelievable that the teachings of this person could be anything else than divinely inspired. He must have reflected that it was impossible for a person who enjoyed exceeding popularity in the whole of Mecca and commanded deep respect from the rank and file of Mecca, to risk the loss of his reputation by upholding the cause of slaves and other depressed classes, unless, of course, this person was acting as the Apostle of the Most High Lord who makes no discrimination between the rich and the poor, the Arab or the non-Arab, free person or slave and who confers His Bounty and Grace upon all His creatures with an even hand. Manifestly these ideas could arise with greater intensity in the minds of slaves than in the minds of free persons. It is due to this reason that the promptness of the slaves' response to the call of the Holy Prophet (peace and blessings of Allah be on him) far exceeded the reciprocation of the free persons with self-styled dignity and honour. The better remained prisoners of their sentiments of racial pride and vanity. The so-called humble and degraded slaves, meanwhile, came forward and achieved such glorious wealth of Faith that posterity will not cease to envy them till the end of the world. The nobles of Mecca had remained behind and had lost this glory, for which they always repented afterwards. Once he had joined the fold of Islam, it was impossible for Bilal (Allah be pleased with him) to renounce his allegiance to faith. No form of tyranny or persecution could shake the firm resolve of this man of deep faith. Faith had permeated through his body and soul. His true happiness lay in the close companionship of his beloved master (peace and blessings of Allah be on him) and in safeguarding the wealth of faith that he had acquired. He wished to augment this wealth at an increasing pace. The tyranny and the savage highhandedness that the infidels committed against him as a reprisal for his allegiance to Islam have been described before. Bilal (Allah be pleased with him) endured all these afflictions with heroic fortitude in order that he might attain tranquillity and serenity of soul. He thus displayed to the world the real significance of true devotion and obedience. Bilal's love and devotion, sincerity and perseverence, determination and fortitude, patience and endurance had inspired sentiments of great respect and adoration for him in the hearts of the most venerable companions of the Prophet (Allah be pleased with them). Impelled by sentiments of deep reverence Haḍrat 'Umar Faruq (Allah be pleased with him) used to remark, "Abu Bakr (Allah be pleased with him) was our chief and ransomed our chief Bilal (Allah be pleased with him)". (Bakhari)

The following episode reveals the high esteem in which Bilal and his companions (Allah be pleased with them) were held by Hadrat 'Umar (Allah be pleased with him). On one occasion Abu Sufyan b. Harb, Suhail b. 'Amr b. Harith and other prominent Arab Chiefs came to the Caliph's court for an interview with Haḍrat 'Umar (Allah be pleased with him). By coincidence Bilal and Suhail (Allah be pleased with them) also arrived. When he learnt of their arrival Haḍrat 'Umar (Allah be pleased with him) called in Bilal and Suhail (Allah be pleased with them) at once while the Arab chiefs, who had come earlier, stood waiting outside. No longer able to restrain himself, Abu Sufyan turned to his companions and remarked, "It was our fate to endure this disgrace. Praise be to Allah, the slaves are admitted to audience while the nobles of Arabia tarry at the door."

Suhail b. 'Amr who excelled Abu Sufyan in strength of faith, on hearing this remark, retorted, "Who is to blame, then? The Caller invited us all with one voice. We refuted the call deeming it as the raving of a mad man and offered severe resistance to him.

On the other hand these slaves went forward and made a positive response. It is their right now to take precedence over us in this world and the next. We have no cause for complaint."

MERITS OF HAḌRAT BILAL

(Allah be pleased with him)

Allah had endowed Hadrat Bilal (Allah be pleased with him) with a righteous nature and he remained true to it till the end of his life. Racial and national traits were fully represented in his character and he was a genuine model of the morals and customs of his nationality.

It was the nature of African slaves that they became deadly foes of their persecutors, but displayed perfect loyalty, sincerity and devotion to those who showed them kindness and fair-dealing and spared no pains in carrying out the commands of good masters.

Haḍrat Bilal (Allah be pleased with him) possessed these virtues to the highest degree. To those who treated him with fairness, he gave his deep loyalty and sincere friendship and to his tormentors he was a dangerous foe. However, he was never the first to start offensive. He never forgot those who had perpetrated atrocities on him and had degraded him. Even in the days of his slavery, when he was completely helpless, he always let it be known to his cruel masters by word and action, that he detested their treatment in his heart. But in view of the tyranny he was made to suffer, how could Bilal (Allah be pleased with him) be expected to give a good account of himself as a slave. Even an ordinary man, who suffers a slight at the hands of another one, begins to nurse a grudge against his persecutor. On the other hand, the very description of the tortures executed on Bilal (Allah be pleased with him) is hair-raising. It was inevitable that these torments produced a reaction in his heart and the deepest contemp he entertained in his soul could not match the crimes of his tormentors. Otherwise, by nature Hadrat Bilal (Allah be pleased with him) was kind-hearted man of righteous faith. Rancour and vendetta were alien to his character. His face was a mirror in which every man could view his own true image. Because of his in-born piety, he possessed the virtues of obedience and true loyalty to the maximum degree. His complete faith in Allah and sincere devotion to the Holy Prophet (peace and blessings of Allah be upon him) revealed how far he had imbibed the good morals of his nation. The sole ambition of his life was to pass his life in the service of the Holy Prophet (peace and blessings of Allah be upon him). He could not bear a moment of separation from the Holy Prophet (peace and blessings of Allah be upon him). After the Prophet (peace and blessings of Allah be upon him) had left for his Heavenly home, Bilal (Allah be pleased with him) had passed the rest of his days in great turmoil of soul in the memory of his beloved master. His earnest longing to wait upon the Holy Prophet (peace and blessings of Allah be upon him) is indicated by the following incident:

When the time of his death approached, his wife, in deep anguish and affliction of soul, began to cry. Noticing her grief, Hadrat Bilal (Allah be pleased with him) remarked: "Why do you weep? You should rejoice at my good fortune. Tomorrow I shall join my companions; tomorrow my eyes shall be blessed with the sight of the Holy Prophet (peace and blessings of Allah be upon him)".

Another prominent trait in Haḍrat Bilal's character was his integrity and credibility. Once he related to his wife a tradition of the Holy Prophet (peace and blessings of Allah be upon him). His wife expressed some doubt as to the authenticity of his report. How could Bilal (Allah be pleased with him) bear anyone casting doubt on his narrative of a tradition? In a mood of high anger, he went to the Holy Prophet (peace and blessings of Allah be upon him) at once and recounted his dispute with his wife. The Holy Prophet (peace and blessings of Allah be upon him) went with him to his house and observed to his wife: "You should take Bilal's word for any tradition of mine, and don't give him cause for anger. He never speaks false". Haḍrat Bilal's credibility was so high among the people that they would rather disbelieve their own eyes than cast doubts on Bilal's report of any tradition of the Holy Prophet (peace and blessings of Allah be upon him). In the Arabian desert where the light of day lingers on after sunset and the glimmer of light is visible even before the hour of daybreak, certain Muslims felt perplexed over the precise times of *iftar* (time of breaking the fast) and *Sahr* (time of commencing the fact). It was Bilal (Allah be pleased with him) who resolved this perplexity of the people during the month of Ramadan. He would come to the mosque and announce that the Holy Prophet (peace and blessings of Allah be upon him) had finished his *Sahr* meal, the people knew that the *sahr* had closed and they stopped eating. Likewise, in the evening when Bilal (Allah be pleased with him) proclaimed that the Holy Prophet (peace and blessings of Allah be upon him) had broken his fast, the people believed the report of Bilal (Allah be pleased with him) and ended their fast. Hadrat Bilal (Allah be pleased with him) paid the greatest regard to truth in all matters concerning the precepts or actions of the Holy Prophet (peace and blessings of Allah be upon him) as well as the affairs of his friends. Once his brother in Islam, Abu Rouwaiha (Allah be pleased with him) wanted to contract marriage with a lady of a certain tribe. Since the suitor was a stranger to the tribe of the bride, he entreated Bilal (Allah be pleased with him) to intercede on his behalf. Bilal (Allah be pleased with him) went with him and testified: "I am Bilal b. Ribah and this is my brother Abu Rouwaiha (Allah be pleased with him), who wants to establish matrimonial connection with you. I must point out, however, that he is a very hot-tempered man. It is up to you to give your daughter in marriage to him or refuse". On hearing this testimony of Bilal (Allah be pleased with him) the parents of the lady accepted the proposal of Abu Rouwaiha (Allah be pleased with him), for they could not disregard the recommendation of Bilal (Allah be pleased with him) in any case. Bilal (Allah be pleased with him) cherished such deep love, sincerity, loyalty and regard for Abu Rouwaiha (Allah be pleased with him) that when Haḍrat 'Umar (Allah be pleased with him) got prepared registers of salaries and allowances, during his caliphate, - he dispatched a communication to Bilal who was with the army in Syria, asking, "Bilal, intimate with whom should we enter thy name"? Bilal (Allah be pleased with him) replied: "Enter my name with Abu Rouwaiha (Allah be pleased with him), whom I shall never abandon on account of the fraternal bond which the Holy Prophet (peace and blessings of Allah be upon him) established between him and me"

This episode indicates two facts. In the first place, Hadrat Bilal (Allah be pleased with him) possessed unfathomable sense of loyalty and deep sincerity and with whomsoever he once struck bonds of amity, he remained faithful and true to his friend till the end of his life. Secondly, he entertained such deep reverence for the Holy Prophet (peace and blessings of Allah be upon him) that he accepted the man whom the Prophet (peace and blessings of Allah be upon him) had made his brother in true faith and treated him as his real brother throughout his life.

One of the most prominent virtues of Hadrat Bilal (Allah be pleased with him) was his integrity and complete honesty. It was on this account that the management of the *Bait-al-Mal* (State Treasury) had been entrusted by the Holy Prophet (peace and blessings of Allah be upon him) to Bilal (Allah be pleased with him). He was also in charge of the household of the Holy Prophet (peace and blessings of Allah be upon him). The Prophet (peace and blessings of Allah be upon him) kept Bilal (Allah be pleased with him) in his train during journeys or in camp. The Holy Prophet (peace and blessings of Allah be upon him) had given the spear which was a present from the King of Abyssinia over to Bilal (Allah be pleased with him) and Bilal (Allah be pleased with him) used to walk ahead of the Holy Prophet (peace and blessings of Allah be upon him) holding this spear on the occasions of Eid and Namaz-i-Istisqa. None among the companions (Allah be pleased with them) enjoyed such close companionship with the Holy Prophet (peace and blessings of Allah be upon him) as Hadrat Bilal (Allah be pleased with him) did. At prayer-time, he used to stand directly behind the Holy Prophet (peace and blessings of Allah be upon him). In the interval between the prayer-timings, he used to attend to the household affairs of the Holy Prophet (peace and blessings of Allah be upon him). He was also responsible for the safe keeping of all the goods received by the Prophet (peace and blessings of Allah be upon him). During journeys, Bilal (Allah be pleased with him) used to pitch the tent of the Holy Prophet (peace and blessings of Allah be upon him) at halting places and improvised a protective shade to his master against the noon-day sun. Bilal (Allah be pleased with him) alone rode on a she-camel ahead of the Prophet (peace and blessings of Allah be upon him). Sometimes, he even enjoyed the privilege of riding on *'Qaswa'*, a she-camel exclusively reserved for the Holy Prophet (peace and blessings of Allah be upon him). No one else except Bilal (Allah be pleased with him) ever dared to ride on this animal. On the eve of victory of Mecca, when the Holy Prophet (peace and blessings of Allah be upon him) entered the Shrine of Ka'ba, he was accompanied by three men only: 'Uthman b. Talha, the key-bearer of the Ka'ba, Usama b. Zaid and Bilal (Allah be pleased with them). Bilal (Allah be pleased with him) remained close at hand even at the time of Prophet's (peace and blessings of Allah be upon him) departure for heavenly home. Hadrat Bilal (Allah be pleased with him) was included among the selected group of few companions who performed the funeral rites of the Holy Prophet (peace and blessings be upon him). When the burial was over, it was Bilal (Allah be pleased with him) who sprinkled water from a skin-bag over the sepulchre of the Holy Prophet (peace and blessings of Allah be upon him). Bilal (Allah be pleased with him) thus gained the rare privilege of administering the last funeral rites of the Holy Prophet (peace and blessings of Allah be upon him).

There was also a psychological aspect to Bilal's deep love and affection for the Holy Prophet (peace and blessings of Allah be upon him . Bilal (Allah be pleased with him), like others of his nation, was an extremist by nature. He loved intensely and hated intensely. He cherished unbounded love for the Holy Prophet (peace and blessings of Allah be upon him) and was deeply devoted to Islam, but he was, at the same time, a staunch foe of the Polytheists of Mecca and he never tried to hide his feelings of hatred and contempt for them. It is proper to bear in mind that hatred, rancour and vendetta are sometimes commendable, though at other times they are certainly reprehensible. If vendetta and animosity against a person are displayed in the way of righteousness and Truth, such conduct is certainly praiseworthy, but if personal conflicts form the basis of enmity and revenge, then these sentiments must be roundly condemned. A bright aspect of Haḍrat Bilal's character is that his vendetta against the Polytheists of Mecca involved no personal feelings. He held the infidels of Mecca in deep contempt because they were the foes of Islam and of the founder of Islam, the

Holy Prophet Muhammad (peace and blessings of Allah be upon him), and also because they had subjected Bilal (Allah be pleased with him) to fearful oppression on the sole ground that he had denounced the religion of his masters and had accepted the call of *Tauhid* (belief in One Allah) and no form of threat or temptation had deflected his steps from the path of fortitude. This extraordinary tenaciousness of purpose was due to his inborn quality of perseverence. This may be illustrated by his firm resolve not to announce the prayer-call after the departure of the Holy Prophet (peace and blessings of Allah be upon him) for his Heavenly home. Somehow he felt convinced in his heart that his recital of the Prayer-call after the Holy Prophet (peace and blessings of Allah be upon him) was no more, would be a breach of loyalty and the pledge of devotion which he had given to his beloved master. Announcement of the Prayer-call apart, Bilal (Allah be pleased with him) found it unbearable to pass his days at Medịna after passing away of the Holy Prophet (peace and blessings of Allah be upon him). He, therefore, earnestly entreated Hadrat Abu Bakr (Allah be pleased with him) to allow him to migrate to Syria to join the Holy War. When Haḍrat Abu Bakr (Allah be pleased with him) showed some hesitation in granting his request, Bilal (Allah be pleased with him) told Haḍrat Abu Bakr (Allah be pleased with him) "If you had paid my ransom for your own sake, keep me; but if you had emancipated me for the sake of the Most High Lord, then permit me to go". In the face of such earnest resolve, Haḍrat Abu Bakr (Allah be pleased with him) was constrained to grant him permission to depart for joining the Holy War in Syria. There is no doubt that it is too much to expect from a man who has himself been a victim of violence and cruelty for a considerably long period to show kindness and consideration to his enemies. Especially in times of war any form of leniency is out of question. Bilal (Allah be pleased with him) was no exception to this general rule and his experience of sufferings and trials had hardened his heart towards the enemy.

At the fall of the Fort of Qamus in the battle of Khyber, Safiyya (Allah be pleased with her), the daughter of the fallen Chief and another girl of tender years were presented to the Holy Prophet (peace and blessings of Allah be upon him). The Holy Prophet (peace and blessings of Allah be upon him) asked Bilal (Allah be pleased with him) to conduct them back to the Fort. Bilal (Allah be pleased with him) led them by the route near which lay the corpses of the slain garrison of the Fort. On seeing this sight, the small girl began to cry in terror. When the Holy Prophet (peace and blessings of Allah be upon him) learnt of this incident, he expressed some displeasure with Bilal (Allah be pleased with him) and said: "Bilal! Have you no compassion? Why did you lead this small girl by the route along which lay the corpses of the slain"? Thereupon Bilal (Allah be pleased with him) replied, "O Prophet of Allah (peace and blessings of Allah be on you), I did not think that you will be displeased. I merely wanted these girls to see with their own eyes the meed of the foes of Allah".

Such an incident had also occurred during the battle of Badr. In the course of the battle, Bilal (Allah be pleased with him) saw Umaiyya b. Khalaf and his son making their escape under the protection of Hadrat Abdur Rahman b. 'Auf (Allah be pleased with him). Both these men used to execute greatest violence upon the Muslims while they lived in Mecca and Bilal (Allah be pleased with him) especially had to suffer the severest torments at their hands. Hence upon seeing these men, Bilal (Allah be pleased with him) at once raised a cry "There goes the Chief of the Polytheists of Mecca. If he escapes from my hands today, I will have done nothing". Bilal's shouting brought several men together. Hadrat 'Abdur Rahman b. 'Auf (Allah be pleased with him) intervened on behalf of the father and son and sustained some injuries in his bid to save their lives. The Muslims cut down the son with sabres. On seeing this, Umaiyya gave out a loud shriek. 'Abdur Rehman b. 'Auf (Allah be pleased with him) was helpless now He said to Umaiyya, "I cannot help you now. Run for your life". But the Muslims did not allow him to escape and killed him with sabres there and then. However, Bilal (Allah be pleased with him) cannot be censured for this occurrence. Umaiyya b. Khalaf deserved this punishment for his heinous deeds. Taking advantage of their helpless state, Umaiyya b. Khalaf had been perpetrating gross violence upon the Muslims as long as they had stayed in Mecca. He was such a cowardly person, however, that on the eve of setting out for the battle, he was at his wit's end for fear of war. Before the battle of Badr, the Holy Prophet (peace and blessings of Allah be upon him) had foretold Umaiyya's end in the battle. As soon as this prediction came to his ears, his face became pale with fear and he began to drag his feet from joining the war. Abu Jahl, the commander of the infidel army, upon learning this, was beside himself with rage. He came to Umaiyya along with few men and handing over a brazier to him remarked, "Sit beside it like a woman and warm your body". This remark stung him and he expressed willingness to set out for the battle. But he displayed no gallantry in war. After a brief engagement when the infidel army fell into disarray, Umaiyya b. Khalaf was the first to fly from the battle. He rushed to his friend from the days of ignorance Hadrat 'Abdur Rahman b. 'Auf (Allah be pleased with him) and besought his protection. When his son was slain in front of him, he felt sure that his own end had come. Seeing the prospect of death before him, he gave out a miserable shriek of fear which cannot be regarded as a befitting behaviour for a gallant man. These incidents testify that Umaiyya was base to the lowest degree. He played a sharp hand in committing violence upon helpless and weak people, yet all his prowess evaporated in a hand to hand fight and he appeared to be a coward of the worst sort. It was for this reason that when Omaiyya was killed, Hadrat Abu Bakr Siddique (Allah be pleased with him) had congratulated Bilal (Allah be pleased with him) by reciting the following verse:

"Felicitation! Bilal!
May Allah bestow all His Grace
upon thee, thou hast taken
vengeance at last".

It should not be, however, construed that Bilal (Allah be pleased with him) was callous. Leaving apart the occasions when the most humane person forsakes leniency.and faces the enemies sternly, Bilal

(Allah be pleased with him) was on all other occasions an extremely affable and humble person. Whenever the people referred to his qualities of patience and fortitude and praised him for his stoic endurance of the worst atrocities in the way of Islam, Bilal (Allah be pleased with him) evinced no pride but cast his head down in humility and said, "I am a very humble person who was a lowly slave till yesterday".

Although Bilal (Allah be pleased with him) had enjoyed a longer period of close companionship with the Holy Prophet (peace and blessings of Allah be upon him) than perhaps any other companion, yet the number of traditions related by him is very few. Except a few *ahadith* concerning prayer, ***Adhan***, breaking of the fast and the commencement of the fast, no other tradition is ascribed to him. This is because he did not like the idea of people sitting in a circle round him and listening to his narration of the *ahadith* with their heads bowed just as a congregation solemnly hears the sermon of the Imam. Haḍrat Bilal (Allah be pleased with him) possessed two other characteristics peculiar to his race: one, deep sensibility; second, love of ease, or in other words, aversion to strenuous or hard labour. Once the Muslims took prisoner the son of a certain man Rayata al–Sahimi. He presented himself before the Holy Prophet (peace and blessings of Allah be upon him) and begged for the release of his son. The Holy Prophet (peace and blessings of Allah be upon him) commanded Bilal (Allah be pleased with him) to go with Sahimi and procure the release of his son. Bilal (Allah be pleased with him) accompanied the man and restored his son to him. On returning, Bilal (Allah be pleased with him) submitted to the Holy Prophet (peace and blessings of Allah be upon him): "O Apostle of Allah, peace and blessings of Allah be upon you, I witnessed a strange sight today. When the father and son were re-united, none of them wept; otherwise on such occasions, people do shed tears of joy". The Holy Prophet (peace and blessings of Allah be upon him) observed: "This is a sign of callousness of the desert Arabs." The above tradition reveals the deep sensibility of Bilal (Allah be pleased with him). Such incidents usually escape the particular attention of a common man, but Bilal (Allah be pleased with him) possessed a peculiarly sharp sensibility. He at once realized that there was something amiss when neither the father nor the son gave way to any expression of joy at their re-union. The incident which illustrates his second characteristic, love of ease, runs as follows:

At the conclusion of the Khyber campaign, the Holy Prophet (peace and blessings of Allah be upon him) proceeded towards the *Wadi al-Qura*. The Prophet (peace and blessings of Allah be upon him) appointed Bilal (Allah be pleased with him) to the duty of waking him up for the morning prayer. The weather was intensely hot. Bilal (Allah be pleased with him) kept awake for a while, but later was overcome by sleep. Since they were all exhausted by the journey, every one overslept and no one rose for the dawn prayer. At last, the Apostle of Allah (peace and blessings of Allah be upon him) rose from sleep. The daylight had broken and the sun had risen in the sky. The Holy Prophet (peace and blessings of Allah be upon him), upon waking up, caused his companions

(Allah be pleased with them) to rise. They startled out of sleep. The Holy Prophet (peace and blessings of Allah be upon him) commanded them to perform ablutions and prayers were said in such condition that the brows of the men were profusely perspiring. When the prayer was over, the Holy Prophet (peace and blessings of Allah be upon him) observed: "Our lives are in the Hand of Allah. The Power to end or prolong our lives is His alone". Afterward the Apostle of Allah (peace and blessings of Allah be upon him) turned to Bilal (Allah be pleased with him) and said: "Bilal! What happened to thee. You promised to wake us all for the morning prayer". Bilal (Allah be pleased with him) submitted: "O Prophet of Allah! May my father and mother be sacrificed for you! My senses were overcome by the same power which seized yours". On hearing this remark, the Holy Prophet (peace and blessings of Allah be upon him) broke into a smile and issued command for the troops to march on. Although it was the only incident of this type, nevertheless, it certainly revealed that Bilal (Allah be pleased with him) possessed some element of indolence.

It was due to his love of ease[1] that not only he himself misses the dawn prayer, in the presence of the Holy Prophet (peace and blessings of Allah be upon him) and his illustrious companions (Allah be pleased with them) but also everyone was delayed in the performance of prayer.

The last tradition which we find about Bilal (Allah be pleased with him) in the history books

(1) This incident, in no way proves th t Haḍrat Bilal (Allah be pleased with him) was ease-loving. It was just an accident that he as overcome by sleep as all others had been overcome. (Translator)

relates to the occasion when Hadrat 'Umar (Allah be pleased with him) had demanded an explanation from Khalid b. Walid through Abu 'Ubaida (Allah be pleased with both of them). Hadrat Khalid b. Walid (Allah be pleased with him) had bestowed a larg purse upon a poet who had written a panegyric. On learning of this event, Hadrat 'Umar (Allah be pleased with him) instructed Hadrat Abu 'Ubaida b. Jarrah (Allah be pleased with him) through a letter to call Khalid in a public assembly and demand an answer from him as to whether he had paid the money from his own pocket or out of the public exchequer. In obedience to this command, Hadrat Abu 'Ubaida (Allah be pleased with him) summoned Khalid (Allah be pleased with him) and confronted him with the question. Khalid (Allah be pleased with him) made no reply. Thereupon Bilal (Allah be pleased with him) came forward and stripping the turban of Khalid tied him up with it. Bilal (Allah be pleased with him) then asked: "Say, whether you gave that sum out of your own pocket or out of the public exchequer of the Muslims"? Khalid (Allah be pleased with him) answered: "I paid the money from my own pocket". On hearing this reply, Bilal (Allah be pleased with him) untied the cloth of the turban from Khalid's neck and rolling it on his head said, "Khalid (Allah be pleased with you), excuse the offense, we have been ordained to obey our leaders in every manner." On careful consideration we find that all actions and deeds of Hadrat Bilal (Allah be pleased with him) revolved round one central point. He had imbibed only one lesson in life and that was to obey his Imam and ruler with utmost devotion and to forget all personal differences to this end. It was for this reason that when he saw Hadrat Khalid b. Walid (Allah be pleased with him) implacable during the inquiry conducted by Hadrat Abu 'Ubaida (Allah be pleased with him), his conscientious and sensitive nature could not bear that a great general should evade answering the question of the *Khalifa-tul-Muslimin* in a public assembly. He stepped forward and tied him up and felt no delicacy about treating a man who was the great Muslim General at the time in such a fashion. However, when Khalid (Allah be pleased with him) gave a satisfactory answer, Bilal's joy knew no bounds. He at once untied the cloth of the turban and rolled it upon Khalid's head and offered his sincere apology by saying that he had not acted out of personal spite, but had wanted to teach the people the lesson of obedience and devotion to their rulers by this example. Bilal's loyalty was reserved for the man who was sincerely and truly devoted to the Commands of Allah and His Apostle (peace and blessings of Allah be upon him). The thought of rendering obedience to his infidel masters had never crossed his mind for a single moment. He had declined to listen to and act upon the orders of his infidel masters at a time when death stared him in the face and he had no hope of surviving their tortures. By such deeds he established a shining precedent of endurance and fortitude which will live forever.

ADHAN

The Call for Prayer

Only such words may suit the call for prayer which spring from the fount of prayer and bespeak the voice of unseen voices veiling the secrets. It is an eternal call which attracts the attention and receives response thereto from the entire universe; and from the moment a man hears the call, he is in a state of prayer and he finds himself in communion with the Unseen. The earth and the heaven resound with the call which blend the awe of the creature with the Exaltedness of Allah. Every time the call is proclaimed, it rejuvenates, in human hearts, an eternal reality which every time sounds as a new reality.

Allah is the Greatest.
Allah is the Greatest.

It is this call with which the believers are summoned to the prayer and it is this very call which is expressive of an eternal reality in an exhaustive manner and wondrous perfection. The repetition of the realities does not cumber the human ears; rather the repetition is indispensible in order to divert human attention from worldly pursuits.

Whenever a Muslim hears the prayer call and he thinks that you call him to the prayer, he is in a state of prayer; for he hymns thereby the Glory of Allah which is the sum and substance of all prayers. The darkness of nights is dispelled by this call as if it were one of the natural phenomena to which ears as well as souls respond; with which the birds and trees stand still; the rivers suspend to flow and wind stops to blow; the entire universe is stirred when the people wake from sleep on hearing the call of the announcer: "Indeed, prayer is better than sleep."

The entire universe sets out in activity. Out of all activities, the prayer is also a light activity; and, verily, the prayer is better than sleep.

When the announcer of the call bids farewell to the day-light and welcomes the dark covers of night, his voice resounds in the atmosphere. It appears as if he delivers a message of life to mankind or bids it to take shelter under the wings of night. It appears as if he makes heavens echo with Allah's Glory and seeks rest in the darkness of night and under the shadows of mysteries and dreams. This prayer-call you would hear at night and in the morning. The call for prayer is heard while the souls are at rest; on hearing it they are startled and engaged in restless struggle. Bodies relax during the night whereas souls are awakened in the daylight. It is a cry which is expressive of calmness and it is a cry that brings out mankind from the hue and cry of the mundane activities:

Hasten to the prayer.
Hasten to well-being.

Yes, it is the only well-being - the great well-being, for all well-being without faith in Allah is out and out a loss.

One cannot appreciate the true import of *Adhan* after separating it from the belief of Islam just as one cannot appreciate anything detaching it from the belief and from the custom and the ways; or just as any stranger cannot at first know about the cities which he has recently visited.

In childhood we hear the *Adhan* but do not understand it, yet when we listen attentively to *Adhan*, we easily distinguish it from the worldly calls, the hue and cry of merriment and the din and bustle of commercial life, catch the spirit of it but we do not know as to how valuable it is. We wish it may prolong and we should hasten to it and respond to the call. All this is done with Allah's Command. We comprehend this word of Command and we comprehend Allah's Word also. But at later stage, this call faints. Thereafter year after year passes away. We attribute it to the amazement of childhood but this state of mind does not change. We suggest different names for this amazement.

There are certain cries and calls which are hidden in one's own self. A man diverts his attention for a moment as he is free from listening these cries. He then turns to the source of call from which it emanates.

The call that will survive in memory is the first call of *Adhan* which is announced to the child for the first time. It never faints from the memory but it is refreshed after a few moments. When a man can recollect the period of his childhood to his leaping, why can't we recollect the past – far or near.

The people who are foreigner to our cities and

ignorant of the faith of Islam, do not comprehend the rites of worship prescribed by Islam as easily as they understand the voice of *Adhan* sounding from the height of minarets, however, variation there may be in the melody and the accepts of the announcer of *Adhan*.

Edward William Lane, the author of the "Manne and Customs of Egyptians" writes, "The call for prayer penetrates into the heart of man. In the still ness of night especially it creates a deep spell". French traveller Gerard E. Nirfal writes in his book "Visits to the East", "In the near East when I heard the sweet melody of the *Muadhdhin's* voice for the first time, I experienced a unique state of enchantment and pleasure. I asked by guide: "What does this man say?" He informed me: "This man announces: "There is no god but Allah". I inquired: "What will he say next"? He replied: "He will proceed to say, "O people who lie in slumber, wake up to offer prayers to the Ever-living Allah who never sleeps."

A Japanese writer Lafcadio Hearn has written a brief article on the First *Muadhdhin* – Hadrat Bilal b. Ribah (Allah be pleased with him). In view of the singular importance of his writing, we shall reproduce a translation of his article in the next chapter. He says: "Travelling through the Islamic lands, if a western tourist happens to pass the night near a mosque with tall minarets, he will hear an enchanting and melodious voice in the calm atmosphere of the dawn. Every word uttered by this voice with its varying rhythm penetrates into the soul and the listener will not fail to be overwhelmed by the spellbinding melody of the announcer of the prayer-call

This is the sound which hearkens the Muslims to offer worship to the one Allah. This call does not only rise in the enchanted atmosphere before dawn, but the tourist will enjoy its sweet symphony four times more till the next dawn. Once at high noon when the horizon is lit by the blazing sun; a second time, just before sunset when the pink rays of the sun illuminate the western horizon; a third time just after dawn when the horizon is drenched in the pale redness of the dying sun and finally when the whole atmosphere is bathed in light and colour and thousands of multi-coloured electric lamps lend on aura of grace and sublime beauty to the yellow domes and tall minarets of the mosques. The listener will hear some additional words in the call which is uttered in the closing watch of the night. If he asks his guide to explain these words, he will get the same answer as Gerard de Nirfal received from his guide. The translator will explain: "Sir, the caller is saying –

> "O thou who lie in slumber! Wake up to offer worship to Ever-living Allah who never sleeps."(1)

In most of the cities of the East, you will see Qur'anic verses inscribed on the stone plates. One of them is: "Touches Him not slumber nor sleep". If the translator is even slightly acquainted with the history of Islam, he will inform the tourist that this call was uttered in the Arabian desert for the first time by an African slave by the name Bilal b. Ribah (Allah be pleased with him), who had the honour of being a close attendant of the Holy Prophet (peace and bless-

(1) The author is referring here to the following words of the prayer-call: (Prayer is preferable to slumber).

ings of Allah be upon him). The Holy Prophet (peace and blessings of Allah be upon him) had entrusted the performance of this call to Bilal (Allah be pleased with him) in preference to a thousand other aspirants. This slave lies buried in the soil of Damascus and his tomb is up to this day the place of visitation where crowds of high and low people come to pay their homage. We have observed with our own eyes foreign tourists who happen to visit our cities, deeply overwhelmed by the sound of the prayer-call.

When they approach near Aswan, they hear the enchanting accents of *Adhan* coming from Cairo and Iskandaria. They mostly hear this *Adhan* in countries other than Islamic States. This call strikes their ears day and night but it does not lose its charm for a single moment; and this is not particularly in the days of congregational prayers.

In the congregational mosques, it is usual for men possessing melodious voices to perform the office of exciting the call and as soon as the call rises, it seems as if a supernatural voice is spell-binding the soul or a melodious bird with its sweet harmony is transporting the audience into a world of ecstasy and enchantment.

The spell which the *Adhan* casts upon the listeners is borne out by the following episode: "In the month of Ramaḍan once the *Muadhdhin* began to beat drums from the tops of the minarets in the small hours of the morning in order to signify to the people that the *Sahri* time had come to a close and hence they should stop taking food or drink. On this occasion some foreign guests in the nearby hotels complained of disturbance in their repose and said to the local authorities that, they deemed that this beating of drums was one of the sacred sign of Islam and when one of them asked about it and they were told that was not one of the signs of Islam but was a convention of the town, they said, "Prayer-Call causes no inconvenience to us. It gives a soothing dream-like sensation to us. But these drums which are played over our heads are a great nuisance to us."

We would have endured this drum-beating, had we known it a sign of Islam which could not be changed. But we have learnt that this custom is changeable in every Muslim country as it suits best its customs and rites. In big cities big drums have been replaced by small ones which are beaten near the doors of the house. Be gracious and guide us to some cities where we may not be disturbed by these drums.

These drums were played for the foreigners during the season of business from arious mounts; the drums were made use of during the period of saints of Sudan for gathering people, or for reminding the unmindful or for the purpose of musical concert. The saints wore such garments and weapons and lived such ways of life that the visitors could easily recognize them in the bazars. They played the small drums with great pleasure because it saved them from the distress of the beating of drums which intermingled with the sonorous voices of the *Muadhdhins.* The beating of drums caused great affliction to them and it marred the beauty of *Adhan* striking the ears of the sleeping people.

In the beginning it was suggested that the Muslims

should be called to prayer by the beating of a drum. The prayer-call had not yet been introduced in the initial stages of Islam. The Muslims were a small minority then and they could be assembled for prayer from the neighbourhood by a call delivered in an ordinary voice. However, after the *Hijra* when the Ka'ba was fixed as the direction for prayers and an ever-increasing number of people joined the fold of islam, the Muslims began to think of a device by which they could be called to prayer from longer distances.The traditions recorded in *Tabqat-i-Ibn-i-Sa'd* and certain other historical records reveal that before *Adhan* was ordained, an announcer appointed by the Holy Prophet (peace and blessings of Allah be upon him) used to ascent a high plane and utter loudly: "The time of congregational prayer has arrived". On hearing this summon people used to assemble in the mosque for the prayer-service. When the *Qibla* was shifted from *Bait al-Maqdis* to the House of Ka'ba, the Muslims felt the need for a device by which people from afar could easily be called together for prayers. Some suggested the blowing of a horn for this purpose. Others recommended the beating of a trumpet; still others put forth the idea that the people should be given the signal for prayer by burning a fire on the top of a mound. But the meeting ended without arriving at a decision. A companion 'Abdullah b. Zaid Khazraji went home still groping for a solution in his mind. His family offered him dinner, but he declined to partake of it and said, "The Holy Prophet (peace and blessings of Allah be upon him) is perplexed over the problem of finding a device for summoning the people to prayer. I shall not eat until I have resolved this question". At night, he had a dream in which he saw a person dressed in a green apparel passing by. The man held a trumpet in his hand. Khazraji (Allah be pleased with him) asked the man, "Will you sell this trumpet?" The man replied: "What will you do with it?" Khazraji (Allah be pleased with him) answered: "I wish to purchase it in order to blow it for calling the Muslims to offer prayer in congregation". The man said, "I shall tell you a better means for achieving this purpose. Instead of blowing the trumpet, you should call out these words:

Allah is the Greatest.
Allah is the Greatest.
I testify that there is no god save Allah.
I testify that Muhammad is the Messenger of Allah.
Hasten to prayer.
Hasten to well-being.
Allah is the Greatest.
Allah is the Greatest.
There is no god save Allah.

This man ascended the top of the mosque and proclaimed these words in a loud voice. Having uttered these words he sat down, for a while and then rising to his feet he said the '*Iqama*' for the prayer which comprised of the same words as those of the *Adhan*.

On waking up 'Abdullah b. Zaid at once presented himself before the Holy Prophet (peace and blessings of Allah be upon him) and delivered to him an account of the occurrence of the night. The Holy Prophet (peace and blessings of Allah be upon him) said to him, "Go to Bilal and make him learn these words by heart. Thereafter Hadrat 'Umar (May Allah be pleased with him) came to the Holy Prophet (peace and blessings of Allah be upon him) and narrated a dream similar to that of 'Abdullah b. Zaid. This is how the *Adhan* was introduced which we hear today. Hadrat Bilal (Allah be pleased with him) made an addition of the following words in the call for dawn prayer:

"The Prayer is better than sleep".

The Holy Prophet (peace and blessings of Allah be upon him) approved of this addition and sanctioned its continued utterance. Hence these words still form part of the call for announcement of *Adhan* for morning prayers. The words "the time of congregational prayer has come" were uttered only on occasions when an assembly of the Muslims had to be convened for consultation upon an important issue or for the public announcement of an important news of victory over the enemy.

There is no difference of views about the text of the *Adhan* among the various sects of Islam. However, the Shi'ites add "Hasten to the best action" with 'Hasten to Prayer" or "Hasten to well-being", and the Malkites say only two in place of four '*Takbirs*'. Similarly, except in the case of the Hunbli Sect, the *Muadhdhins of* all sects make it a point to deliver the words of the *Adhan* in a rhythmical and melodious strain so as to enchant the hearts of the listeners and the prayers with eagerness and zest. The Apostle of Allah (peace and blessings of Allah be upon him) entrusted Bilal (Allah be pleased with him) with the duty of proclaiming the call for prayer five times a day, and the people heard the recital of the prayer-call for the first time in his voice. No other person among the Muslims could attain that honour save Bilal (Allah be pleased with him) and he could take legitimate pride on this singular honour. Over and above that, he enjoyed the grand privilege of holding the office of *Muadhdhin* in a mosque where the Holy Prophet (peace and blessings of Allah be upon him) himself led the prayer-service.

The sayings of the companions (Allah be pleased with them) reveal that Hadrat Bilal (Allah be pleased with him) possessed a harmonious voice. His recital of of the prayer-call produced a peculiar state of spiritual solemnity and reverence in the souls of the Muslims. As soon as his call arose in the air of Medina, each person was impelled to invoke benediction on him and every living soul in Medina began to recite, 'I testify that there is no deity except Allah. I testify that Muhammad is the Apostle of Allah.' The traditions which date from after the victory over Mecca report that the Polytheists of Mecca sorely detested the voice of Bilal (Allah be pleased with him). They used to enquire from each other, "Did Muhammad (peace and blessings of Allah be upon him) find no other man except this slave who raises his shrill voice from the top of the Ka'ba". In their wildest thoughts they could never have imagined a slave getting to the top without hestitation and announce prayer-call whereas a man from the noblest Arab tribe could not dare ascend the roof of the Ka'ba and desecrate it. Some of the Polytheists on viewing this sight said to Harith b. Hisham. "Do you see where this slave stands"? Hisham gave a polite reply and parried the question by saying, "Leave him to his own self. If Allah disapproves of it, He will put a stop to it". On the day when the Holy Prophet (peace and blessings of Allah be upon him) commanded Bilal (Allah be pleased with him) to ascend the roof of the Ka'ba and recite the prayer-call from there, Harith b. Hisham, Abu Sufyan b. Harb and 'Uttab b. Usaid were seated in the courtyard of the Ka'ba. When they heard the voice of Bilal (Allah be pleased with him). 'Uttab said: "Allah was exceedingly kind to Ussaid that He removed him from the world before this day, for had he heard these words, he would not have survived". Harith b. Hisham confessed: "By Allah! Had I known that Muhammad was true, I would have followed him". Abu Sufyan deposed: "I will not say anything, for if I utter anything these pebbles will report my words to Muhammad". As a matter of fact, the Polytheists of Mecca naturally abhored the prospect of any one, even an angel climbing the roof of the Ka'ba and proclaiming the Oneness of Allah. They found such a call from the top of the Ka'ba utterly insufferable. The unseemly words that they used with reference to Hadrat Bilal (Allah be pleased with him) were uttered because the proclamation of the sovereignty of One Allah was being made from the roof of the Ka'ba, although before this, three hundred and sixty idols had reigned in the same House of Ka'ba. Secondly, this proclamation was being made by a man who was an extremely humble and a lowly person in their estimation and who had been the victim of their savage tortures during his former stay in Mecca.

The real cause for the Meccans' anger was that

Bilal (Allah be pleased with him) had a powerful voice and his call vibrated all quarters of Mecca and the proclamation of the creed of One Allah was heard by every citizen. We need not bother to draw a contrast between the reverence and love that *Adhan* produced in the hearts of believers and the enmity which was roused in the hearts of Polytheists, for the Holy Prophet (peace and blessings of Allah be upon him) had selected him; he called the Prophet and the Muslims and his call was heard five times a day. Had his voice lacked melody and harmony, the Holy Prophet (peace and blessings of Allah be upon him) who was endowed with a high aesthetic sense, would not have selected Bilal (Allal be pleased with him) for this office. This was the same proclamation which the Meccans had endeavoured to suppress with all their might and main as a sequel to which the Holy Prophet (peace and blessings of Allah be upon him) was constrained to migrate with his companions (Allah be pleased with them) to the sanctuary of Medina, three hundred miles distant from Mecca.

THE FIRST MUADHDHIN OF ISLAM

Several works have been produced in the European languages on the biographies of the Caliphs (Allah be pleased with them) and other companions of the Holy Prophet (peace and blessings of Allah be on him) who were destined to play the part of righteous Caliphs and eminent rulers. But scanty material is available about those companions (Allah be pleased with them) who did not take part in the political affiars or were not appointed to important offices of the State. Hadrat Bilal (Allah be pleased with him) belongs to this latter group. Hence the volume of writings about Bilal (Allah be pleased with him) is very small. Among the few European authors who have produced some writings on Hadrat Bilal (Allah be pleased with him), Lafcadio Hearn is the most famous. Hearn has written an article in English on Hadrat Bilal (Allah be pleased with him). For some time Hearn worked as a journalist in the American Press. Later he spent sometime in Indo-China. He, then, travelled around several Asian countries and finally settled down in Japan for good. He married there and devoted himself to academic and literary pursuits concerntrating his mind on mysticims of the East, no matter what its source was – Arabia, China or Japan. Lafcadio Hearn's essay is worthy of being presented to the readers in translation, for it shows the deep impression made by the sincere and faithful character of Hadrat Bilal (Allah be pleased with him) on the minds of prominent shcolars, who have a philosophic out look of life. Hearn begins his essay with a brief quotation of verse from the English poet Edwin Arnold, in which the poet addresses the Lord in this manner:

Even if such a day comes to pass when this world shall be empty of Thy worshippers and no sound rises in Thy praise from any corner of the earthly planet, even then emblems of Thy Existence shall be visible in every direction of the universe and every inch of the earth will bear witness to Thy Being All planets in the sky that rotate day and night and all the stars which illuminate the world with their Heavenly glow are Thy disciples who orbit around Thy luminous Heavens rendering praise and homage to Thee."

Having quoted these verses Hearn proceeds to write–

Bilal (Allah be pleased with him) was an African slave. But his name has become external by virtue of his strength of faith, love and devotion to the Holy Prophet (peace and blessings of Allah be on him), and for his melodious voice. The call which he pronounced in the desert of Arabia has been repeated in the same form by every *Muadhdhin* of Islam for the last twelve hundered years. The prayer-call which is proclaimed to-day from the desert of Morocco to the extreme boundaries of the Far East comprises of the same words which were first recited by the toungue of

Bilal (Allah be pleased with him). The possession of certain attributes is considered essential for a *Muadhdhin*. For instance, he must be Hafiz Qur'an i.e. he must have committed the whole text of the Qur'an to memory. (This is not a necessary qualification of a *Muadhdhin* in Islam.) He should be free from all taint of vice. He must posses a clear and resonant voice. His accent must be cultured. He should be able to deliver the correct phonetic sound of the words. Apart from all these, the most essential qualification of a *Muadhdhin* is that he should have a melodious voice capable of producing a sensation of pleasure in the souls of the listeners. The renowned Persian poet Musleh-ud-Din Sa'di Shirazi in his work 'Bostan' has recorded some interesting tales which reveal the extent of importance attached by Muslims to the harmonious delivery of *Adhan*. One of these tales reocrded by Sa'di runs as follows:-

In Sanjar there lived a *Muadhdhin* whose voice was so coarse that everyone despired to listen to him. The *Mutawalli* (Caretaker of the Mosque) was a good-natured man. He did not wish to injure the feelings of the *Muadhdhin* by sacking him outright. He, therefore, employed a subtle device to get rid of him. One day he called the *Muadhdhin* and said to him, "Before thee, we had two *Muadhdhin* to announce the call in this mosque and each one of them was paid a sum of five dirham as honorarium. They are now imploring me for jobs again. I suggest you take ten dinars from me and leave the service of this mosque. Go somewhere else so that these poor men may find means of employment." The *Muadhdhin* agreed to this condition and having received ten dinars departed to some other place. Not long afterwards he presented himself before the *mutawalli* (caretaker of the Mosque) and said– "Master you deprived me of announcing the Call in your mosque on payment of ten dinars. I went to another place and the people said to me, "If you leave our mosque we will pay you ten dinars in consideration of your acceptance of our proposal." But I understood their motive and emphatically declined to relinquish my office of proclaiming the *Adhan*."

When the *mutawalli* heard this, he broke into a smile and said, "If you insist on staying there and refuse to submit to any pressure, those people will soon agree to pay even fifty dinars to secure your departure."

Sheikh Sa'di has narrated another tale of a similar type. He writes– "A *hafiz* of the Qur'an used to recite the Qur'an in a very coarse voice. A man once passed near him and enquired– "What are thy wages for reciting the Qur'an?" The *hafiz* replied, "I get nothing fot it." The man remarked, "Why do you undertake such labour and strenuous work without being paid for it." The *hafiz* replied, "I do it for the sake of Allah." The man thereupon said, "If you have Allah's favour in view, the only means you can win it is by refraining from reciting the Qur'an."

Bilal (Allah be pleased with him) began his life as a slave, for he was born of a black slave girl. Little information about his childhood days is available. According to the description recorded by Sir William Muir, Bilal's complexion was jet black. He had thick hair. His features proclaimed him to be born of negro race. He was tall, thick – set and possessed nerves of steel.

The initial call of the Holy Prophet (peace and blessings of Allah be on him) made a deep impression on the slaves of Mecca. This helpless class, which was groaning under the yoke of the worst system of slavery, found in the teachings of the Holy Prophet (peace and blessings of Allah be on him) the soothing effect of a balm, as it were for their festering sores. Bilal (Allah be pleased with him) was the first among his countrymen to accept Islam. It was with reference to this fact that the Holy Prophet (peace and blessings of Allah be on him) had observed, "Bilal is the first fruit of Abbysinia." Bilal (Allah be pleased with him) must have unconsciously imbibed the lesson of believing in one Allah from his mother during his childhood. In the 4th century A.D. the christian doctrine in Abbysinia was dominated by the belief in one Allah. Bilal (Allah be pleased with him) must have assimilated these teachings through his mother. It was due to this early, upbringing that he unreservedly accepted Islam when the Call of the Holy Prophet (peace and blessings of Allah be on him) came to him.

The poor and depressed class of the slaves was the especial target of the atrocities of the Polytheists of Mecca. It was an ancient custom of the Arabs that they guarded the lives of their friends and relative at the cost of their own lives. They gave their lives, but never allowed anyone to molest a person whom they had pledged protection. A man who murdered his enemy could seldom succeed in saving his own life from the vengeance of the murdered man's family

Sometimes endless blood feuds were opened on the murder of a single person and generation after generation, the conflicting parties perished in the fight. It was on this account that Muhammad (peace and blessings of Allah be on him) and such of his companions, who were free citizens of free tribes untramelled by the claims of slavery, were immune from violence and murderous attacks to some extent. They belonged to tribes and their tribes, according to the ancient custom, were under obligation to wreak vengeance for any violence perpetrated on them But the helpless slaves enjoyed no such protection. They were an open target of heinous tortures. They were stripped naked and stretched on the burning sand in the blazing heat of summer. While in this state, heavy stones were placed upon their chests. They were dragged over the stony ground of Mecca and by inflicting these tortures, the Polytheists coerced them to denounce Muhammad (peace and Blessings of Allah be on him) and his divine creed. Many slaves succumbed to these tortures and were compelled to utter blasphemies which suited the views of their cruel masters. They were also made to confirm their denunciation of Islam by swearing on al-Lat and al-Uzza. The Apostle of Allah (peace and blessings of Allah be upon him) comforted these powerless and helpless people and set their souls at rest by observing that if they remained truly devoted to their creed, their faith was beset with no danger.

The Holy Qur'an also refers to these people in the following words:-

> "It is only those, who believe not in the signs of Allah, who fabricate lie. And they, they are the

liars. Whosoever disbelieveth in Allah after his belief – save him who is constrained and his heart is at rest with the belief – but such as open their breasts to disbelief, on them is Allah's wrath and for them is a severe torment." (Qur'an: 16: 105, 106)

In this period of suffering Bilal (Allah be pleased with him) remained firm in his devotion to Islam. He did not utter a syllable derogatory to the honour of the Holy Prophet (peace and blessings of Allah be upon him) under the most unbearable atrocities. Lashing, fire burns, excruciating pangs of hunger and thirst could not weaken the resolve of this most devoted of men. No form of tryanny and oppression could deflect this man of iron faith from his loyalty to Islam. The tortures of the Polytheists of Mecca could only elicit the words 'Ahad, Ahad' (Allah is one and He has no partner) from him.

The renowned Persian poet, Farid ud Din 'Attar in his book *'Mantiq ut Tair,* has referred to Bilal's fortitude in the following terms:–

> "Bilal's poor body received such heavy strokes of sticks and lashes that his skin was badly off and his wounds bleeded profusely, yet he remained adamant in the open proclamation of the creed of one Allah."

It so happened one day that this black slave was as usual suffering torment at the hands of his master. When a frail, short but broadfaced man of handsome features passed by. This frail person was a noted business-man of Mecca 'Abdullah b. 'Uthman

Abi Qahafa' who is known as Abu Bakr (Allah be pleased with him) in the annals of Islam. He was a close friend of the Holy Prophet (peace and blessings during the journey when they migrated from Mecca to Medina. On this occasion they had taken refuge in a cave. It is reported that when the Prophet (peace and blessings of Allah be on him) and his friend entered the cave a spider wove a web at the opening of the cave. When the pursuers reached the mouth of the cave, they found it covered with the web. Thinking that had anyone entered the cave, the web would have been broken, they stopped there and did not enter the cave. Abu Bakr (Allah be pleased with him) was the father of 'A' isha (Allah be pleased with her), the beloved wife of the Holy Prophet (peace and blessings of Allah be on him). Abu Bakr (Allah be pleased with him) himself received the distinction of becoming the first Caliph after the demise of the Holy Prophet (peace and blessings of Allah be on him).

In the initial period of Islam, Abu Bakr (Allah be pleased with him) was an extremely wealthy person. He was a man of deep compassion and could not bear to see the miserable plight of the slaves. He, therefore used to spend a considerable portion of his wealth on purchasing freedom for these slaves. He gave a total of about forty thousand dinars in ransom for all these slaves who were subjected to atrocities by their owners in reprisal for their devotion to Islam. A considerable number of these male and female slaves were old and weak. Abu Bakr's father Abu Qahafa disapproved of his buying old and inform slaves and women and used to say, "If you must buy slaves, you should bargain for strong and sturdy men who may be useful to you and may aid and protect you in the time of need." But Abu Bakr (Allah be pleased with him) would answer, "Father, I do not buy them for my own use. I purchase them to win the favour of Allah and my purpose in paying their ransom is to emancipate them from the yoke of slavery." It is related that the personal habit of this man, who spent thousands of dirhams in the manumission of slaves, was to put on an apparel woven out of goats' hair or thick and coarse cloth. When Abu Bakr (Allah be pleased with him) saw Bilal (Allah be pleased with him) being subjected to cruel tortures, he could not bear the sight. He struck a bargain with Umaiyya b. Khalaf and Abi b. Khalaf, the owners of Bilal (Allah be pleased with him) and purchased him on payment of a robe and ten dinars. Who could predict then that one day the same Umaiyya and his son who were perpetrating severe tortures upon Bilal (Allah be pleased with him) would be prostrate before their former slave imploring mercy and forgiveness, but their entreaties would be spurned. This day came before a decade was over and both tormentors perished at the hand of Bilal (Allah be pleased with him) in the battle of Badr.

In former days Bilal (Allah be pleased with him) whom Abu Bakr (Allah be pleased with him) purchased and set free, was really a very useful and energetic slave. He had a strong constitution and his cruel masters, therefore, used to exact heavy labour from him. Abu Bakr (Allah be pleased with him) used to purchase the freedom of the slaves in order to win the favour of Allah, but who can restrain the wags?

The slanderers with a view to defaming Abu Bakr (Allah be pleased with him) said that he had purchased slaves with profit motive. This notion of the people has been alluded to in the *'Sura al-Lail'* of the Holy Qur'an in the following terms:–

> "By the night when it envelops
> (the world) and the day when the
> light is in full glow. And by
> the creation of male and female (as
> witness to the fact) that thy efforts
> are indeed diverse. Hence to him
> who spends in the way of Allah and
> cultivates piety and affirms what
> is righteous, We shall certainly
> afford moments of ease; and to him
> who is stingy and displays indifference
> and refutes what is righteous we shall
> send affliction upon him and his wealth
> will not avail him at the time of death.
> To provide guidance in the world
> is truly Our responsibility and We have
> power over the beginning and
> end of everything. So
> remember I give you warning of
> a raging fire. None but the
> most wicked shall enter it – such
> a one as refuted the truth and
> turned his face from it. He who
> is devoutly pious shall certainly
> be kept far away from the Fire –
> such a one as spends his wealth
> in the way of Allah, so that he may
> attain purity of soul and wishes
> not to do favour to any one to
> obtain advantage in return, but his
> motive is to win the favour of the
> Most High Lord and the Lord will
> surely be pleased with him."
> (92: 1–22)

After obtaining his freedom, Bilal (Allah be pleased with him) became a close, confidant and devoted attendant of Muhammad (peace and blessings of Allah be upon him) and worked zealously with the Prophet (peace be upon him) in the task of the propagation of Islam. It is reported in some traditions that Bilal (Allah be pleased with him) had returned to Mecca after the *Hijra* (migration to Medina). When the Quraish of Mecca detected him, they arrested Bilal (Allah be pleased with him) and put him to severe tortures. But this tradition is unreliable and is not corroborated by the authoritative works on the History of Islam. After the year of *Hijra*, he returned to Mecca only in the company of the Holy Apostle (peace and blessings of Allah be upon him) and not before. The *Hijra* (emigration) to which we refer here, was the migration to Medina, which the Muslims of Mecca undertook in obedience to the command of the Holy Prophet (peace and blessings of Allah be upon him). The Muslims had at that time taken refuge in Medina to escape the atrocious persecution of the Quraish. Bilal (Allah be pleased with him) had accompanied the other Muslims in their journey from Mecca to Medina, and there we would see Bilal (Allah be pleased with him) performing the office of the first *Mu'adhdhin* of Islam.

In the early days of the advent of Islam, people were unaware of the idea of *Adhan.* At that time the Muslims formed a small group who lived in the immediate neighbourhood of the house of the Holy Prophet (peace and blessings of Allah be upon him). Hence they could easily assemble for the prayers. A man used to stand and make a loud call and the people immediately arrived to form a congregation. Even after the *Hijra,* the need for the introduction of a regular prayer-call was not felt until the building of the mosque of the Prophet (peace and blessings of Allah be on him) and the charge of the direction from *Bait-al-Maqdis* to Mecca and the Ka'ba.

It is stated that one of the signs of the Hour of Resurrection is, that Christ at the time of his descent at the mosque, will turn his face towards *Bait-al-Maqdis* at the time of morning prayer. The mosque will be illuminated by his divine glow. He will step to the *Mehrab.* The people will think that this all is due to him. But he will announce, "There is no god save Allah and Muhammad is his Messenger."

How did the idea of the *Adhan* arise? It is a fascinating story which may be stated briefly as follows:–

After the *Hijra* when the *'Masjid-i-Nabvi'* was completed, the Apostle of Allah (peace and blessings of Allah be on him) decided that the existing device of calling the Muslims to prayer service was unsuitable to the prevailing circumstances, for it lacked the solemn dignity which should be an essential characteristic of a Call to assemble the people in a congregation for prayer. The Holy Prophet (peace and blessings of Allah on him) at first thought of using a horn for the purpose of inviting people to the prayers, but he (peace be on him) later dropped the idea, for the blowing of a bugle was the custom of the Jews and the Apostle of Allah (peace and blessings of Allah be on him) did not wish to adopt any Jewish custom after the change of the direction of the prayers towards the Ka'ba. Subsequently, the Holy Prophet (peace and blessings of Allah be on him) considered the possibility of using a trumpet for this purpose, but no workman was available at that time in Medina who could manufacture a trumpet, Meantime a citizen of Medina had a dream in which he saw a tall person standing in the moonlight near his house. He was clad in a green apparel and held a beautiful trumpet in his hand. The dreamer approached this man and offered to buy the trumpet. The man smiled and enquired, "Why do you want to purchase this trumpet?" The dreamer replied "I wish to buy it on behalf of the Holy Prophet (peace and blessings of Allah be on him) so that he may put it to use for calling the Muslims to prayer." The tall man answered– "Let me give you a better suggestion. Instead of blowing the trumpet, a man should ascend the roof of the mosque and announce the call for prayer in the manner I announce before you." So saying the man plugged his ears with the finger tips and recited those words with such deep melody and excellent rhythm creating a celestial awe in the heart of a man which would be heard five times during the day in every Muslim habitation from the Shores of Africa fo the Indo-Pakistan Sub-continent upto the present day.

"Allah is the Greatest"
"Allah is the Greatest"
"I testify that there is not God except Allah"
"I testify that Muhammad is the Apostle of Allah."

When the dreamer woke up these words were still

resounding in his ears. He came to the Holy Prophet (peace and blessings of Allah be upon him) at once and related his dream. The Holy Prophet (peace and blessings of Allah be upon him) listened to this dream as attentively as he used to listen to the true dreams bringing the guidance from Allah. The Prophet (peace and blessings of Allah be upon him) summoned his loyal and sincere attendant, Bilal (Allah be pleased with him) and asked him to announce loudly from the roof of the mosque at the time of each prayer the words heard by that pious man in his dream. It was the closing watch of the night. In obedience to the command Bilal (Allah be pleased with him) ascended the roof of the mosque and started calling the people to assemble in the mosque for prayers in his typical harmonious voice. As soon as the half-awake people heard the enchanting and attractive voice of Bilal (Allah be pleased with him), they rose from their beds in astonishment and having made hurried preparations, reached the mosque for the prayer service. Even today, beautiful minarets of the mosques can be seen everywhere in the world of Islam. The *Mu'adh dhins* ascend the top of these minarets five times a day and announce the call for prayer. The original conception of these minarets dates back to twelve hundred years from the time when Bilal (Allah be pleased with him) climbed the roof of the mosque and his announcement of the *Adhan* resounded the atmosphere of Medina. During this long span of twelve hundred years, hardly a day has passed when the Call of *Adhan* has not been announced from any corner of the world of Islam. One of the chief advantages of *Adhan* is that it announces the exact hour of the day to the residents of every community and they can easily regulate the hours of their daily business in accordance with the prayer – timings. The devout eagerness with which Muslims converge upon the mosques for offering devotion to the One Allah immediately on hearing the prayer – call is really amazing. Sometimes this prompt zeal for attending the mosque for prayer has been the cause of untold suffering for the Muslims. For instance at the time of the invasion of Changez Khan the Muslims were caught in a trap in Nishapur, the beloved town of the famous poet'Attar and for the first time, in the history of Islam, people came to realize that *Adhan* could be used to inveigle the people into a treacherous snare.

In the year 608 H, the array of Changez Khan invaded Nishapur. Changez Khan's name has become a symbol of ruin and devastations. He has never been matched in acts of bloodshed and cruelty. It was a custom with him to assault a city and then retreat. When sometime had elapsed and the population returned to their homes in the city and resumed their daily occupation, Changez Khan would attack on them unaware. By this strategy, the people, who had survived the first attack, were easily entrapped the second time and were instantly destroyed by Changez Khan's troops. In keeping with this custom, when Changez Khan launched a second attack upon Nishapur, he adopted the device of sending his own troops to go to the mosque and proclaim the *Adhan* in order to assemble the citizens in one place. As soon as the Call of 'Allah - O -Akbar', 'Allah is the Greatest' arose, crowds of people began to congregate in the mosques. Changez Khan's troops were lying in

weariness of the journey. However, one man among them possessed a dull soul. He had no interest in music, nor in mystical verse. When we reached the oasis of the tribe of Bani Hilal, we saw a black slave inside the tent of a bedouin Arab. He was reciting certain verses in such a melodious strain that it seemed as if the heavens had opened and a bird of the paradise was spell-binding the universe with its sweet ditties. Strangely that dull companion of ours appeared to be unaffected by the enchanting voice of the singing slave. As the slave continued to sing, the camel of that man overthrew its wooden saddle and ran loose towards the desert. Thereupon I reprimanded the man in a high tone, "Woe be to thee: A wild and mute beast was so affected by the music of this slave's voice that it broke loose, but in spite of being a human being you remained so insensitive:

In his *'Tarikh - ul - Khulafa'*, Maulana Jalal ud Din Suyuti has recorded the following episode. "Salim, the camel driver of the Abassid Caliph Mansur, once during a journey so enchanted the Caliph by his musical recital, that the Caliph narrowly escaped a fall from the camel. Immensely pleased, he gave a reward of half a dirham to the singer.

On receiving this paltry sum, Salim Said., "You have betstowed on me only half a dirham. I once made a performance of a similar song before the Ummayid Caliph, Hisham bin Abdul Malik, and he had conferred a bounty of ten thousand dirhams on me."

In short, during the days of ignorance and in the early period of the advent of Islam the black slaves or their offspring formed the majority of singers. Nature had endowed them with a deep flair for rhythm and they were masters of musical strains. They reached the peak of glory in making musical instruments. Bilal (Allah be pleased with him) was a black slave too and like other slaves his voice must have been exceedingly melodious. It was by virtue of this that the office of announcing the prayer - Call was conferred on him. There is, however, one moot point to be resolved. Was the style of *Adhan* (which was emulated by *Mu'adh dhins* in later ages) introduced by Bilal himself or had this style been ordained to him by the Holy Prophet (peace and blessings of Allah be on him)?.

In this connection it is noteworthy that although the ancient Arabs had a taste for music, yet they had no knowledge of the intricacies and principles of the art of music. They certainly appreciated music, yet lacked the accomplishment to play it. Since Bilal (Allal be plased with him) was a slave and had been grazing camels in the days of his slavery there is no doubt that he was wellversed in the art of music and in songs sung to accelerate the speed of camels. It is probable, therefore, that when 'Abdullah b. Zaid Khazraji (Allah be pleased with him) came and related his dream to the Holy Prophet (peace and blessings of Allah be on him) and the Holy Prophet (peace and blessings of Allah be on him) asked Bilal (Allah be pleased with him) to ascend the roof of the mosque and announce the prayer-Call, Bilal (Allah be pleased with him), in keeping with his musical nature, recited the words of the call so melodiously that the Holy Prophet (peace and blessings of Allah be on him) highly approved of the style and ordained its continuance as he had ordained that the words الصلوٰة خير من النوم (Prayer is better than sleep) should continue to be delivered in the same strain in which Bilal (Allah be pleased with him) had first recited them at the hour of morning prayer.

It is highly improbable that 'Abdullah b. Zaid (Allah be pleased with him) had heard a particular style of announcing the *Adhan* and after awaking from the dream would have repeated the words of the *Adhan* in the same rhythmical strain before the Holy Prophet (peace and blessings of Allah be on him). As we have written before the Arabs were not versed in this art and were incapable of rendering musical tunes with their own tongues even when they had heard them.

Bilal (Allah be pleased with him) continued to serve the Holy Prophet (peace and blessings of Allah be on him) till the end. Soon after announcing the Call for dawn prayer, he would go to the door of the Holy Prophet (peace and blessings of Allah be on him) and would wake him by reciting a verse from the Qur'an. When the congregation had assembled in the mosque, all eyes were turned towards this slave, who would stand in the first row behind the Holy Prophet (peace and blessings of Allah be on him). As soon as Bilal (Allah be pleased with him) had said the *Takbir*, the Holy Prophet (peace and blessings of Allah be on him) would commence the prayer, Bilal (Allah be pleased with him) rose in importance and dignity with the increase in power and glory of Islam. Several other important duties were entrusted to him besides the office of announcing the *adhan*, he was the keeper of the Prophet's (peace and blessings of Allah be on him) household. He also served as Treasurer of all the wealth received on account of *'Zakat'* and *'Sadaqat'* On the eve of the victory over Mecca, when the Holy Prophet (peace and blessings of Allah be on him) rode on his She-Camel to the door of the Ka'ba, he (peace be on him) received the keys from the keeper of the Ka'ba and gave them over to Bilal (Allah be pleased with him). The Holy Prophet (peace and blessings of Allah be on him) then commanded Bilal (Allah be pleased with him) to open the door of the Ka'ba. On this historic occasion it was Bilal (Allah be pleased with him) who gained the singular honour of ascending the roof of the Ka'ba and announcing prayer - call from there. Bilal's love and devotion to his master was so deep, that he always remained in attendance on him during journeys or in camp. It was Bilal's duty to raise a canopy of cloth over the Holy Prophet (peace and blessings of Allah be on him) to shield him from the glare of the sun.

After the demise of Muhammad (peace and blessings of Allah be on him), the sweet recital of the night - ingale of Islam was no more to be heard. Some other *Mu'adhdhins,* therefore, began to perform the office of announcing the prayer - call when Bilal (Allah be pleased with him) had voluntarily abdicated the office.

Bilal (Allah be pleased with him) had resolved never to recite the call for any other Imam after the passing away of his beloved master. We do not know for how long Bilal (Allah be pleased with him) remained in the company of Abu Bakr (Allah be pleased with him) after the demise of the Holy Prophet (peace and blessings of Allah be on him). There is absolutely no doubt, however that none in Medina enjoyed as much honour and esteem as did Bilal (Allah be pleased with him). His high status can well be assessed by the fact that he sent a message for marriage on behalf of his brother Abu Rouwaiha to an Arab family. The family and ancestral pride of the Arabs is proverbial. The very thought of giving their daughters in marriage to slaves is anathema to them. Yet despite this pride, they felt such deep reverence for Bilal (Allah be pleased with him) in their hearts, that they offered no objection to giving their daughter in marriage to Bilal's brother, and set aside all the considerations of pedigree.

It is recorded in certain traditions that after the reign of the first Caliph (Allah be pleased with him), Bilal (Allah be pleased with him) was assigned some state duties. When,' Umar b al Khattab (Allah be pleased with him), whose name had become a legend for his stern justice and equity – called upon Khalid b. Walid – Saif Allah –(Allah be pleased with Him) – to explain his conduct in connection with some of his alleged irregularities and errors, it was Bilal (Allah be pleased with him) who took off Khalid's turban from his head and tied his hands with it in open assembly and did not untie him until Khalid (Allah be pleased with him) had furnished a satisfactory explanation of all the charges framed by the Chief of the believers – the Caliph. However history contains no noteworthy record of his life, after this episode, except the detail that he had joined the Muslim army in the Holy War in Syria. He hac completely dissociated himself from public life in the closing phase of his life. He acquired a piece of land in the environs of Damascus and passed his days in peace and isolation.

The Chief companions (Allah be pleased with them) had departed this world. Abu Bakr, Khalid and *mujahidin* of Islam (Allah be pleased with them) had joined their master, the Holy Prophet (Peace and blessings of Allah be on him) in the Eternal Garden. The affairs of Muslim Government were now largely in the hands of these who had not seen the days of the Prophet (peace and blessings of Allah be on him).

The vast extension of Muslim conquests had brought in such abundance of goods and wealth, that it appeared as if rivers of gold were converging on Medina. The new generation lacked the qualities of their predecessors. They forsook the bedouin simplicity which was the hall mark of Arab life and took to a luxurious and comfortable way of life. Hadrat Umar (Allah be pleased with him) was a man of foresight. He had a deep awareness of this situation. On several occasions he fell into weeping on the apprehension lest this abundance of goods and wealth should sow the seeds of wickedness among the Ummah, and the passions of jealousy and enmity aroused by material wealth should throw the state into chaos.

Meanwhile the Religion of Islam, in reprisal for devotion, to which Bilal (Allah be pleased with him) used to suffer tortures day and night and the number of followers of which had remained limited to a few members of the tribe of Abu Talib – had crossed the expanse of land and Sea and held sway over Syria, Palestine and Persia, Bilal (Allah be pleased with him) himself did not live to see the vast expansion of the empire of Islam, but his descendants witnessed the glorious scene when the echo of prayer – call *(adhan)*, which their forebearer had first announced in the rocky plain of Medina, was heard from the boundaries of India to the shores of Atlantic Ocean. Bilal (Allah be pleased with him) had given up announcing the *adhan* after the demise of his beloved master. He cherished such deep love for the Holy Prophet (peace and blessings of Allah be on him), that he could not bear the thought of announcing the Call – which he used to announce especially for the Prophet (peace be on him) and in response to which the Prophet (peace be on him) would arrive for the prayers – for anyone else after the demise of the Holy Prophet (peace and blessings of Allah be on him,).

During his stay in Medina and Syria, people made entreaties to him on several occasions to announce the *Adhan,* but he invariably declined. However when Hadrat 'Umar (Allah be pleased with him) visited Damascus, and in view of the great desire of the troops, requested Bilal (Allah be pleased with him) to deliver the *Adhan*, Bilal (Allah be pleased with him), in deference to the wishes of the *Amir – ul – Mu'mineen,* complied with the request and this was the final Call of Bilal's life time.

As soon as the news got around that Bilal (Allah be pleased with him) would announce the Call for dawn prayers, a great surge of excitement rose among the troops. Everyone rushed towards the mosque in a frenzied state of mind, for it was after a long period of time that they were about to receive the privilege of listening to the prayer-call in the voice of the *Mu'adhdhin* of the Holy Prophet (peace and blessings of Allah be on him).

Traditions relate that as soon as Bilal's voice vibrated through the air waves and resounded in the atmosphere, it produced a state of great commotion in the congregation. The people recalled to their imagination the times when the Holy Prophet (peace and blessings of Allah be on him) was alive and Bilal (Allah be pleased with him) used to recite the prayer-call standing before the chamber of the Prophet (peace and blessings of Allah be on him). History records that the whole congregation in the mosque dissolved into sobs and lamentation on that occasion. Haḍrat 'Umar (Allah be pleased with him) and the bravest of the warriors of Islam who had remained unruffled in the most terrible moments of war and had not displayed any wavering of spirit on the most fearful occasions, not gave way to emotion; and unable to maintain patience and self-composure burst into uncontrollable weeping until their beards were drenched with tears.

Would that there were a device in those times by which Bilal's peculiar form of recital could be recorded and preserved so that we in modern times could also listen to the melodious tunes which so enthralled the people of the early period of Islam.

We have no reliable means for concluding as to what extent the style of the Prayer – Call adopted by the present day *Muadhdhins* is modelled on the style of Bilal's recital. Yet, since the Arabs are well known for their custom of preserving their religious heritage, it is quite possible that through generations they may have maintained intact the same form of recital of the *Adhan* which their forebears had learned from Bilal (Allah be pleased with him).

It is especially noteworthy that the Jews have preserved some of the *'Ibrani'* musical songs in their original style of recital since the times of Haḍrat Sulaiman (peace be on him) and they have won remarkable success in this endeavour. If the Jews can succeed in maintaining a musical tune for thousands of years, why can't the Arabs? Hence it is not beyond possibility that the present rhythmical form of recital of the *Adhan* is the same as was originated by Bilal (Allah be pleased with him).

FINALE

In the preceding Chapter we have presented a translation of Lafcadio Hearn's essay on Haḍrat Bilal (Allah be pleased with him). The readers will have noted that the essay reveals considerable affection on the part of the author for his subject and he has drawn an attractive picture of Haḍrat Biblal (Allah be pleased with him). However, despite his great reverence and probity Lafcadio Hearn has not succeeded in avoiding certain errors in his essay. His errors, nevertheless, do not stem from any dishonest motives similar to other orientalists, but are unintentional and are due merely to his inadequate knowledge and understanding of the subject. In view of the importance of the topic we consider it obligatory to correct these errors.

The first grave mistake of the author relates to his mention of the offspring of Haḍrat Bilal (Allah be pleased with him). As *Ibn – i – Hisham* has clearly reported Haḍrat Bilal (Allah be pleased with him) begot no child. All other historical works are also silent on this point. Another error committed by the author is that he has referred to Haḍrat Abu Rouwaiha (Allah be pleased with him) as the real brother of Bilal (Allah be pleased with him). The most authoritative traditions establish the fact that Abu Rouwaiha (Allah be pleased with him) was not the blood brother of Bilal (Allah be pleased with him). Bilal and Abu

Rouwaiha (Allah be pleased with them) had been made brothers unto each other when the Holy Prophet (peace and blessings of Allah be on him) had established the bond of brotherhood between the *muhajireen* (emigrants) and the *Ansar* (Local Supporters. Hearn has also alleged in his essay that the Arabs were ignorant of the art of music, because their tongues could not utter certain sounds in proper fashion. It was for this reason that the majority of singers in Arabia consisted of foreign slaves and slave-girls, who were free from any such deficiency. But this argument is untenable. The Arab nation exists to this day and we are well aware of the fact that their tongues can utter all forms of sounds in a correct manner. It is true that they did not display much interest in singing or playing the music. They considered music to be the pastime of women. The Arabs were traders and a warlike race. They, therefore, did not appreciate a noble man indulging in any thing except vigorous life in both winter and summer seasons. They spent most of their time in journeys, battles and internecine wars. They disapproved of any member of their tribe renouncing the bedouin character and the arduous and strenuous occupations of life and devote himself to singing and playing the music. It was due to this reason that singing and the performance of music was limited to the class of female slaves, slaves and hermaphrodites and the majority of musicians belonged to the slave class. Otherwise the voices of the Arabs did not lack artistic finesse. One proof of this is songs of camel – drivers as the custom of singing songs to drive fast the camels is very popular among the Arabs and the art of camel driving is closely related to the science of music.

In the stillness of the night when the light of the moon sheds lustre over the atmosphere, the songs of the bedouin Arabs, while they drove camels, transport the listeners into raptures. However it should not be inferred from this explanation that the Holy Prophet (peace and blessings of Allah be on him) had appointed Bilal (Allah be pleased with him) to the office of the announcer of the Prayer-Call because of his accomplished knowledge of the intricacies and rules of the art of music.

It is possible that Bilal (Allah be pleased with him) had been engaged in grazing the camels and had acquired deep knowledge of the art of a camel-driver's songs during his travels to the Yemen and Syria from Hejaz. But there is no tradition which tells us that, like other slaves, he was engaged in the occupation of singing or playing music either before or after the advent of Islam.

In actual fact the people knew the high pitch of Bilal's voice in peace and war and the songs that he sung on journeys. It was on this account alone that the Holy Prophet (peace and blessings of Allah be on him) had entrusted him with the duty of announcing the Prayer-Call. Considering his exceeding piety, devotion to worship and regular attendance in the mosque, the choice of the Holy Prophet (peace and blessings of Allah be on him) naturally fell on him for the performance of this important duty and Bilal (Allah be pleased with him) acquitted himself with deep sincerity and extraordinary devotion.